McGraw Hill

T0022859

500
SAT Math Questions
to know by test day

McGraw Hill

500
SAT Math Questions

to know by test day

Third Edition

Anaxos, Inc.

New York   Chicago   San Francisco   Athens   London
Madrid   Mexico City   Milan   New Delhi
Singapore   Sydney   Toronto

1 2 3 4 5 6 7 8 9   LCR   26 25 24 23 22 21

ISBN   978-1-264-27780-3
MHID   1-264-27780-6

e-ISBN   978-1-264-27781-0
e-MHID   1-264-27781-4

SAT is a registered trademark of the College Board, which was not involved in the production of, and does not endorse, this product.

Anaxos, Inc. has been creating education and reference materials for over fifteen years. Based in Austin, Texas, the company uses writers from across the globe who offer expertise on an array of subjects just as expansive.

McGraw Hill products are available at special quantity discounts to use as premiums and sales promotions or for use in corporate training programs. To contact a representative, please visit the Contact Us pages at www.mhprofessional.com.

CONTENTS

INTRODUCTION

Congratulations! You've taken a big step toward SAT success by purchasing *McGraw Hill 500 SAT Math Questions to know by test day*. We are here to help you take the next step and score high on your SAT exam so you can get into the college or university of your choice!

This book gives you 500 SAT-style multiple-choice questions that cover all the most essential material. The questions will give you valuable independent practice to supplement your regular textbook and the ground you have already covered in your math class. Each question is clearly explained in the answer key.

This edition features our 20-question diagnostic quiz at the beginning of the book to test your knowledge up front. Designed to represent the different topics covered on the SAT, it can give you a head start on learning what you know and what you need to improve upon.

This book and the others in the series were written by expert teachers who know the SAT inside and out and can identify crucial information as well as the kinds of questions that are most likely to appear on the exam.

You might be the kind of student who needs to study extra a few weeks before the exam for a final review. Or you might be the kind of student who puts off preparing until the last minute before the exam. No matter what your preparation style, you will benefit from reviewing these 500 questions, which closely parallel the content, format, and degree of difficulty of the math questions on the actual SAT exam. These questions and the explanations in the answer key are the ideal last-minute study tool for those final weeks before the test.

If you practice with all the questions and answers in this book, we are certain you will build the skills and confidence needed to excel on the SAT. Good luck!

—*Editors of McGraw Hill*

THE SAT DESIGN

Test Categories

The test is broken down into the following four sections, with more emphasis on algebra as the foundation for all other mathematics and less emphasis on geometry and trigonometry. At the beginning of each section of practice questions in this book, you will find a description of the topics covered on the test, skills that will be tested, and need-to-know topics including formulas and definitions.

Section I: Heart of Algebra
- linear equations
- systems of linear equations
- equations and inequalities to represent relationships between quantities and solve problems
- using graphs to solve problems

Section II: Problem Solving and Data Analysis
- ratios, proportions, percentages, and units
- linear and exponential growth
- probabilities
- using statistics to determine mean, median, mode, range, and standard deviation
- table data, scatterplots, data collection, and inferences

Section III: Passport to Advanced Math
- equivalent algebraic equations
- quadratic formulas
- nonlinear equations
- graphing exponential, quadratic, and nonlinear functions
- polynomial factors

Section IV: Additional Topics in Math
- area and volume
- theorems related to lines, angles, triangles, and circles
- right triangles
- trigonometry

Calculator/No-calculator Sections

The test will be given in two parts. The first part of the math test is a no-calculator section. This section contains questions that test basic mathematical skills, recall of common formulas, and strategy skills. The second part of the test is the calculator section. This test will include questions similar to part one, but it will also include questions that require more advanced mathematical operations. It is important to note that the SAT calculator section is designed to test the use of the calculator as an appropriate tool to be used when necessary; however, many questions do not need a calculator. Using a calculator may not be the most efficient strategy, and students will have to determine whether or not it would be helpful for a particular question.

Open-Ended Questions

On each part of the test, there will be open-ended questions that do not have multiple-choice answers. Students will need to solve these problems and record their answers on the answer key in a grid. It is important to remember the following things:

- The answers will NEVER be negative numbers, only positive numbers or zero.
- The grid can only hold four decimal places so record answers as accurately as possible, rounding when required.
- Fractions do not need to be reduced to their lowest terms.
- Mixed numbers need to be converted to improper fractions before being recorded in the grid.

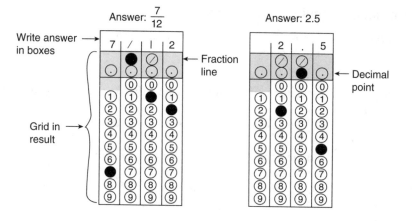

Write answer in boxes

Fraction line

Grid in result

Answer: $\frac{7}{12}$

Answer: 2.5

Decimal point

Answer: 201
Either position is correct.

Acceptable ways to grid $\frac{2}{3}$ are

Information Provided on the Test

The SAT test does provide you with some helpful information at the beginning of each test in a Notes section.

Notes:
1. The use of a calculator is **permitted/not permitted (depending on which section)**.
2. All variables and expression used represent real numbers unless otherwise indicated.
3. Figures in the test are drawn to scale unless otherwise indicated.
4. All figures lie in a plane unless otherwise indicated.
5. Unless otherwise indicated, the domain of a given function f is the set of all real numbers for x for which $f(x)$ is a real number.

The test also includes geometry formulas for reference, which may be helpful, particularly for Section 4.

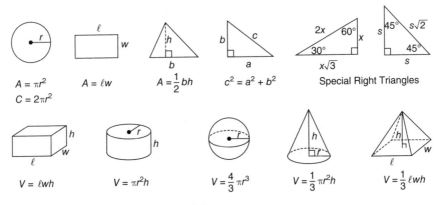

$A = \pi r^2$ $A = \ell w$ $A = \frac{1}{2} bh$ $c^2 = a^2 + b^2$ Special Right Triangles

$C = 2\pi r^2$

$V = \ell wh$ $V = \pi r^2 h$ $V = \frac{4}{3} \pi r^3$ $V = \frac{1}{3} \pi r^2 h$ $V = \frac{1}{3} \ell wh$

The number of degrees of arc in a circle is 360.
The number of radians of arc in a circle is 2π.
The sum of the measures in degrees of the angles of a triangle is 180.

McGraw Hill

500
SAT Math Questions
to know by test day

DIAGNOSTIC QUIZ

Take this 20-question quiz to get a sense of where you are in your studying. The questions have been chosen to represent the different topics covered on the Math portion of the SAT. They are designed to match the latest SAT style and format. Check the answers and explanations at the end of the quiz.

1. The mean of the data set $[x^1, x^2, x^3, x^4, x^5, z^1, z^2, z^3]$ is 5. If the mean of the data set $[z^1, z^2, z^3]$ is 10, then what is the mean of $[x^1, x^2, x^3, x^4, x^5]$?
   (A) 1
   (B) 2
   (C) 3
   (D) 4

2. Suppose $x = \dfrac{2}{5^{-2}}$ and $y = \dfrac{3}{2^{-1}}$. What is the value of xy?

   (A) $\dfrac{6}{50}$
   (B) $\dfrac{6}{25}$
   (C) 2.4
   (D) 300

3. If $3x - 5 = 4$, then what is the value of $2x - 2$?
   (A) 3
   (B) 4
   (C) 5
   (D) 6

4. Ana decided to open a bakery that sells brownies and lemon tarts. During her first day of business, she earned $300 by selling 15 brownies and 10 lemon tarts. During her second day, she earned $831 by selling 24 brownies and 55 lemon tarts. What is the price of her brownies?
   (A) $9
   (B) $10
   (C) $12
   (D) $14

5. If $2x^2 + 8y = 32$, then what is the value of $\frac{1}{2}x^2 + 2y$?

(A) 2
(B) 4
(C) 8
(D) 12

6. Suppose that a, b, c, and d are real nonzero numbers. If $d = \frac{ab}{c}$ and $b = \frac{c}{a}$, then which of the following is equivalent to d?

(A) 1
(B) a
(C) c
(D) $\frac{a^2}{c^2}$

7. Kronhorst International has a marketing division and a sales division. The marketing division has 23 employees, and the sales division has 18 employees. There are 9 employees who work in both of these departments. How many employees work in only one department, and how many employees work in only the marketing department?

(A) 5 and 12
(B) 23 and 9
(C) 23 and 18
(D) 41 and 9

8. The probability of event A taking place is $\frac{x}{3}$, and the probability of event B taking place is $\frac{2x}{5}$. These events cannot take place at the same time. What is the probability of either event A or event B taking place?

(A) $\frac{x}{15}$

(B) $\frac{2}{15}$

(C) $\frac{11x}{15}$

(D) $\frac{2x^2}{15}$

9. Consider a data set that has 10 values. Each value is 8 more than the previous value. If the largest value is 109, then what is the median of this data set?

    (A) 54.5
    (B) 65
    (C) 71
    (D) 73

10. What is the probability that a randomly generated three-digit integer will be less than 200 and divisible by both 6 and 9?

11. A university has 10 members of a chess club, 15 members of a soccer club, and 20 members of a basketball club. No one is a member of more than a single club. From the pool of people involved, what is the chance of selecting a member of either the chess club or the soccer club?

    (A) $\dfrac{2}{9}$

    (B) $\dfrac{1}{3}$

    (C) $\dfrac{4}{9}$

    (D) $\dfrac{5}{9}$

12. Assume that x and y are real numbers. Which of the following would be equal to 25% of $8x + 20y$?

    (A) $\dfrac{8x + 20y}{25}$

    (B) $\dfrac{2x + 5y}{4}$

    (C) $2x + 5y$
    (D) $4x + 10y$

13. Which of the following is identical to $a^2b^5 + ab^2 - a^2b$?

    (A) $ab\left(ab^4 + b - a\right)$
    (B) $ab\left(ab^4 - b + 1\right)$
    (C) $a\left(ab^4 + ab - ab\right)$
    (D) $a^2b\left(b^4 + b - 1\right)$

14. What is the smallest possible value of x that can make the equation $3x^2 - 13x = 10$ correct?

15. If $f(x)$ is the function shown here, then which of the following would be $f(x) + 2$?

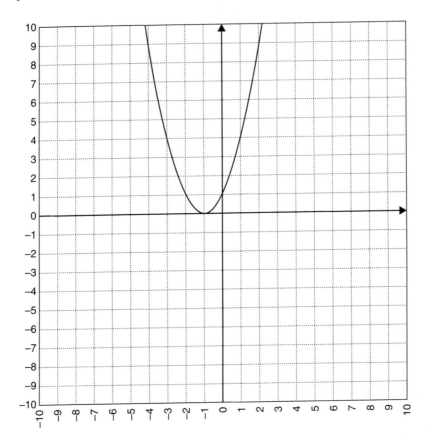

(A)

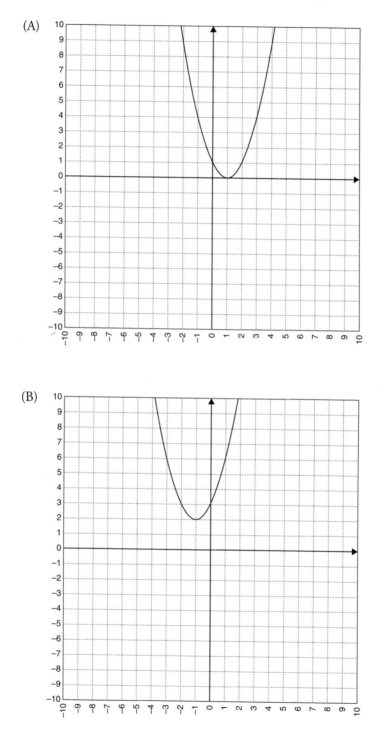

(B)

(C)

(D)

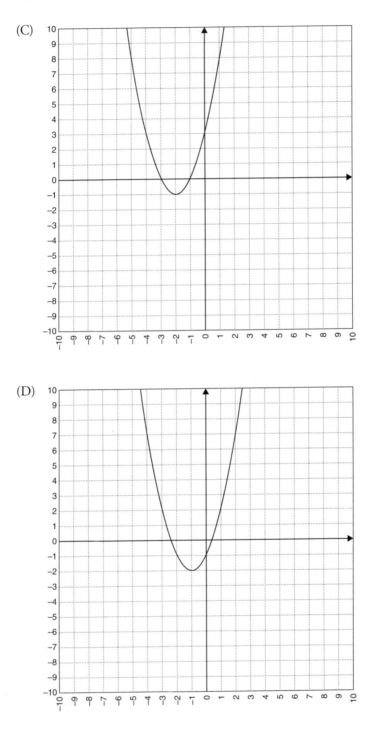

16. The point $(6, y)$ lies on the chart $6x^2 - x^3 + 2$. What is the value of y?

(A) −3
(B) 0
(C) 2
(D) 6

17. The value of the function f can be found by squaring the difference between that number and 5 and then subtracting 10. Which of the following is $f(x)$?

(A) $x^2 - 5$
(B) $x^2 - 5x - 5$
(C) $x^2 + 10x + 10$
(D) $x^2 - 10x + 15$

18. Triangle ABC (shown here) is a right triangle. The value of the angle CAD is 118 degrees. What is the value of the angle ACB?

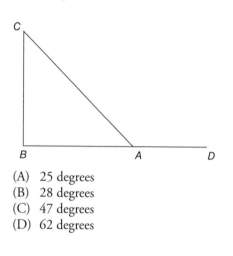

(A) 25 degrees
(B) 28 degrees
(C) 47 degrees
(D) 62 degrees

19. For triangle ABC (shown here), the value of angle BCD is equal to 30 degrees. If CD is the height of the triangle and is 12 centimeters, then what is the perimeter of triangle ABC?

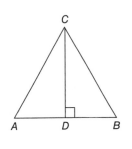

(A) $6\sqrt{3}$

(B) $9\sqrt{3}$

(C) $\dfrac{21\sqrt{3}}{2}$

(D) $18\sqrt{3}$

20. If $\sin \alpha$ is $\dfrac{3}{14}$ and $\cos \alpha$ is $\dfrac{2}{7}$, then what is the value of $\tan \alpha$?

(A) $\dfrac{3}{49}$

(B) $\dfrac{3}{4}$

(C) $\dfrac{13}{14}$

(D) $\dfrac{7}{4}$

DIAGNOSTIC QUIZ ANSWERS

1. **(B)** The total value of the sum of $[z^1, z^2, z^3]$ is the number of values times the mean. Because there are 3 values, this means that the value is $10 * 3 = 30$. The same can be applied to the entire data set $[x^1, x^2, x^3, x^4, x^5, z^1, z^2, z^3]$ that has 8 values, meaning that the sum of its values is $5 * 8 = 40$.

It can then be calculated that the mean $[x^1, x^2, x^3, x^4, x^5, z^1, z^2, z^3] =$
$$\frac{30 + 5 * \text{mean}\,[x^1, x^2, x^3, x^4, x^5]}{8} = 5$$
This means that $30 + 5 * \text{mean}\,[x^1, x^2, x^3, x^4, x^5] = 40$.

If $5 * \text{mean}\,[x^1, x^2, x^3, x^4, x^5] = 10$, then the mean is 2.

2. **(D)** The response is equal to $2 * 5^2$ for x and $3 * 2$ for y, meaning that the total value is $50 * 6$, which is equal to 300.

3. **(B)** If $3x - 5 = 4$, then this means that $3x = 9$. Then, it can easily be calculated that $x = 3$. This leads to $2 * 3 - 2$ ultimately having the value of 4.

4. **(D)** This is most easily solved from a system of equations. Brownies are represented by x, and lemon tarts are represented by y. Two basic equations are based on the money earned during the first 2 days of Ana's business:

$15x + 10y = 300$
$24x + 55y = 831$

By multiplying the first equation by 5.5, we can infer that $82.5x + 55y = 1650$. The second equation is then multiplied by -1. Then, we can summarize these equations to infer that

$58.5x = 819$
$x = \dfrac{819}{58.5} = \$14$

5. **(C)** The second equation is divided by 4, meaning that the final result is 32 divided by 4, which is equal to 8.

6. **(A)** If $b = \dfrac{c}{a}$, then we can input this value instead of c into the first equation. By doing so, we find that $\dfrac{a * c}{c * a}$, meaning that the value is 1.

7. **(B)** Because there are 9 employees who work in both divisions, there are $(23 - 9) + (18 - 9)$ employees working in either the sales department or the marketing department. This amounts to 23 employees. The total number of individuals working only in marketing is $18 - 9 = 9$.

8. **(C)** The two probabilities just need to be summed, which can be developed as $\dfrac{5x}{15} + \dfrac{6x}{15}$. This is equal to the option offered in answer choice (C).

9. **(D)** If the largest value is 109, then the data set will be [37, 45, 53, 61, 69, 77, 85, 93, 101, 109]. Then, the median should be $69 + 77$ (or $109 + 37$). When either sum is divided by 2, the final correct value will be 73.

10. $\left(\text{Grid-in answer} = \dfrac{1}{150}\right)$

    There are 900 three-digit integers, but only 100 of them are smaller than 200. Of those 100, any one that is a multiple of 18 will be divisible by both 6 and 9. There are 6 such values; the smallest of which is 108 and the largest of which is 198.

    The probability of such a number being generated is $\dfrac{6}{900} = \dfrac{1}{150}$.

11. **(D)** There are two ways to solve the problem. The total number of individuals is 45.
    The probability of selecting a member of the chess club is $\dfrac{10}{45}$. The probability of selecting a member of the soccer club is $\dfrac{15}{45}$. The probability of selecting a member of the

    basketball club is $\dfrac{20}{45}$. The answer can be calculated by summing the probabilities of selecting a member of the chess and soccer club: $\dfrac{2}{9} + \dfrac{1}{3}$.

    Another way to calculate the correct answer would be to subtract the chance of picking a member of the basketball club from 1. This would lead to $1 - \dfrac{4}{9}$ and the same accurate response of (D).

12. **(C)**

    This can be easily calculated as $\dfrac{25}{100}(8x + 20y) = \dfrac{1}{4}(8x + 20y) = 2x + 5y$

13. **(A)** It can be calculated that $ab(ab^4 + b - a) = a^2b^5 + ab^2 - a^2b$. Answer choice (B) is incorrect because ab^2 is positive, not negative. The final two answer choices are also inaccurate because of at least one of the elements of the equation.

14. $\left(\text{Grid-in answer} = \text{answer} = \dfrac{2}{3}\right)$

    The equation can be rewritten as

    $3x^2 - 13x - 10 = 0$

    $= (3x + 2)(x - 5)$

    The solutions are $\dfrac{2}{3}$ and 5, with the first one being the smallest possible value of x.

15. **(B)** If the function shifted as $f(x) + 2$, then this would mean it moves up by 2. This is represented in answer choice (B).

16. **(C)** The answer can be calculated by entering $6 * 6^2 - 6^3 + 2$. This is equal to 2.

17. **(D)** This answer can be calculated by entering the equation $f(x) = (x - 5)^2 - 10$. This translates to $x^2 - 10x + 25 - 10 = x^2 - 10x + 15$.

18. **(B)** If the value of the angle CAD is 180 degrees, then we can infer that the value of the angle CAB is $180 - 118 = 62$ degrees. Because the triangle is a right triangle, the value of the angle CBA is 90 degrees. Therefore, the value of the required angle is $180 - 90 - 62 = 28$ degrees.

19. **(D)** Based on the fact that the angle of BCD is equal to 30 degrees, we can infer that the value of the final angle of either triangle ACD or triangle BCD is $180 - 30 - 90 = 60$ degrees. Because the value of the angles of triangle ABC is 60, this means that triangle ABC is equilateral.

Based on that assumption, we can use the formula for height $= \dfrac{a\sqrt{3}}{2}$, which gives us the value of one side as $6\sqrt{3}$. Then, the final value of the perimeter is the value of the side multiplied by 3 (because this is an equilateral triangle), meaning it is $18\sqrt{3}$.

20. **(B)**

The equation is as follows: $\tan \alpha = \dfrac{\sin \alpha}{\cos \alpha}$

$$= \dfrac{\dfrac{3}{14}}{\dfrac{2}{7}}$$

When this expression is rationalized, the correct answer choice is (B).

Heart of Algebra

On the SAT Math test, the Heart of Algebra section represents the largest percentage of the test. Algebra is consistently present throughout most high school math courses and is a prerequisite for moving on to higher-level mathematics in postsecondary education and career applications. The test presents both straightforward questions and questions that require more in-depth interpretations and problem-solving strategies.

Topics

- Linear equations and inequalities
- Systems of linear equations
- Equations and inequalities to represent relationships between quantities
- Graphs

Skills

- Solve linear equations and inequalities.
- Use multiple steps to simplify expressions and equations or solve for a variable.
- Use equations and inequalities to solve problems.
- Use graphs to solve problems.
- Identify relationships between equations and graphs.

Need to Know

- Equation of a line: $y = mx + b$

- m is the slope: $m = \left(\dfrac{\text{Rise}}{\text{Run}}\right) = \dfrac{(y_2 - y_1)}{(x_2 - x_1)}$

- b is the y-intercept

- Midpoint formula: $\left(\dfrac{(x_1 + x_2)}{2}, \dfrac{(y_1 + y_2)}{2}\right)$

- Distance formula: $\sqrt{\left[(x_2 - x_1)^2 + (y_2 - y_1)^2\right]}$

Questions 1–54 should be answered without a calculator.

1. When 21 is divided by j, the remainder is 3. If j is less than 9, what is the remainder when 30 is divided by j?
   (A) 0
   (B) 2
   (C) 5
   (D) 6

2. Suppose $m = 3*8^{-2}$ and $n = 5*8^{-2}$. What is the value of $m - n$?

   (A) $-\dfrac{1}{2084}$

   (B) $-\dfrac{1}{32}$

   (C) $-\dfrac{1}{16}$

   (D) $-\dfrac{1}{8}$

3. If $x = -1$, which of the following is the least in value?
   (A) $-x^{-1}$
   (B) x^{-2}
   (C) $-2x^{-2}$
   (D) $2x^{-2}$

4. There are 19 students enrolled in a history class and 24 students enrolled in a physics class. If 7 students are enrolled in both courses, how many are enrolled in only one of the courses?
   (A) 43
   (B) 36
   (C) 29
   (D) 28

5. Suppose the remainder when x is divided by 3, 4, or 11 is 0. Which of the following numbers must x be a multiple of?
   (A) 6
   (B) 8
   (C) 16
   (D) 47

6. If $n^4 = 144$, what is the value of n^2?

   (A) 12
   (B) 36
   (C) 72
   (D) 288

7. Suppose a, b, and c are positive real numbers. Which of the following expressions is equivalent to $14a = b^2c^6$?

   I. $a = \dfrac{(bc^3)^2}{14}$

   II. $14a = (bc^4)^2$

   III. $ab^{-2} = \dfrac{c^6}{14}$

   (A) I only
   (B) II only
   (C) I and II only
   (D) I and III only

8. Suppose m, n, and p represent numbers such that $-1 < m < 0 < n < 1 < p$. Which of the following has the smallest value?

   (A) mn
   (B) mp
   (C) np
   (D) n^2

9. If $m = \left(\dfrac{p}{q}\right)^2$ and $n = \left(\dfrac{q}{p}\right)^{-2}$, what is the value of $\dfrac{m}{n}$?

   (A) -1
   (B) 1

   (C) $\left(\dfrac{p}{q}\right)^2$

   (D) $\left(\dfrac{p}{q}\right)^6$

10. Suppose m is an odd integer greater than 10. What is the remainder when m is divided by 2?

11. Suppose $j = \dfrac{1}{4^{-2}}$ and $k = \dfrac{3}{2^{-1}}$. What is the value of jk?

(A) $-\dfrac{3}{16}$

(B) $\dfrac{3}{32}$

(C) $\dfrac{3}{2}$

(D) 96

12. If $a < 0$, then which of the following must also be less than 0?

  I. $\dfrac{-1}{a^3}$

  II. $a + 10$

  III. $2a^{-1}$

  (A) I only
  (B) II only
  (C) III only
  (D) I, II, and III

13. Which of the following expressions is equivalent to $\left(\dfrac{2}{3} m^3 n^{\frac{1}{2}} \right)^2$ for all integer values of m and n?

(A) $\dfrac{4}{9} m^6 n$

(B) $\dfrac{2}{3} m^6 n$

(C) $\dfrac{4}{9} m^5 n^{\frac{5}{2}}$

(D) $\dfrac{2}{3} m^5 n^{\frac{5}{2}}$

14. If $3^{4a} = 9^{3b}$ and the value of a is 2, then what is the value of a?

15. If $\left|-(-x)^2\right| = 9$, what is a possible value of x?

(A) -3

(B) $-\dfrac{1}{9}$

(C) 6

(D) 9

16. If $3x^2 + 6x = 18$, then what is the value of $\dfrac{x^2}{2} + x$?

(A) 2

(B) 3

(C) 6

(D) 9

17. The sum of two consecutive integers is 75. What is the value of the smaller integer?

(A) 24

(B) 29

(C) 37

(D) 41

18. If $4ab = 24$, what is the value of $(2ab)^2$?

(A) 24

(B) 48

(C) 144

(D) 576

19. Which of the following expressions best represents this statement? "The difference of two numbers is 7 less than the sum of the same two numbers."

(A) $a - b = a + b - 7$

(B) $a - b - 7 = a + b$

(C) $a - b = ab - 7$

(D) $a - b - 7 = ab$

20. If for an integer a, $3x^2 = 2a$, then what is the value of $(3x - a)(3x + a)$ in terms of a?

(A) $3a^2$

(B) $9a^2$

(C) $2a + a^2$

(D) $6a - a^2$

21. Bobby is 6 years older than Gina, and Gina is 4 years older than Ann. How many years older than Ann is Bobby?

    (A) 4
    (B) 6
    (C) 10
    (D) 14

22. Company A has a profit that is three times larger than that of company B. Company B's profit is the square root of that of company C, which earned $2,500 in profit. What is the profit of company A?

    (A) $50
    (B) $150
    (C) $833.33
    (D) $18,750,000

23. A student sets his budget for electricity at x. If for each of n days he uses k worth of electricity, which of the following expressions represents the amount left in his budget?

    (A) $x - n$
    (B) $x - k$
    (C) $nx - k$
    (D) $x - nk$

24. A company rents graphing calculators for $15 a month for the first 3 months and then $10 for each of the following months. If a student rents a calculator for 9 months, how much will she pay in rental fees?

    (A) $60
    (B) $90
    (C) $105
    (D) $135

25. The sum of two positive numbers is 28, and the difference of the same two numbers is 16. What is the value of the product of the two numbers?

26. If $x^2y^3 = 128$ and the value of y is 2, then what is the highest possible value of x?

    (A) 2
    (B) 4
    (C) 6
    (D) 8

27. Consider a series of numbers in which the first number is 3 and each additional number is two times the value of the original number but subtracted by 2. What would be the value of the 10th number in this series?

    (A) 67
    (B) 131
    (C) 259
    (D) 515

28. Which of the following values of x satisfy the inequality $-5 < 2x < 7$?

    (A) -3
    (B) -2
    (C) 4
    (D) 7

29. If a, b, x, and y are positive numbers such that $a = 2x + 4y$ and $b = x + 2y$, how many times larger than b is a?

    (A) 1/2
    (B) 1
    (C) 2
    (D) 4

30. Let $x \oplus y = \dfrac{x + y^2}{x}$ for all nonzero values of x and all real values of y.

    Which of the following is equivalent to $(2xy) \oplus (4xy)$?

    (A) $9x^2 y^2$
    (B) $16x^2 y^2$
    (C) $1 + 2xy$
    (D) $1 + 8xy$

31. 15 is the sixth and largest number in a series of six consecutive odd numbers. What is the second member of the series?

    (A) 5
    (B) 7
    (C) 9
    (D) 11

32. A store clerk earns \$11.50 per hour before taxes. Next year, the clerk will be given a raise of \$1.25 each hour. If she works h hours per week, which of the following represents her weekly wage after the raise?

    (A) $12.75h$
    (B) $11.5h + 1.25$
    (C) $11.5 + 1.25h$
    (D) $\dfrac{12.75}{h}$

33. If $-\dfrac{2}{3}a \geq 1$, which of the following is a possible value of a?

    (A) $-3/2$
    (B) $-1/3$
    (C) $2/3$
    (D) $4/3$

34. If $\dfrac{3x+6}{5} = \dfrac{2x+5}{3}$, then what is the correct value of x?

    (A) -9
    (B) -7
    (C) -2
    (D) 5

35. A certain spice mixture stays fresh for 3 months. A restaurant purchased 3 pounds of the mixture last month and 2 pounds this month. If the spice mixture is stored and not used, how many pounds will still be fresh in 4 months?

    (A) 0
    (B) 1
    (C) 3
    (D) 5

36. What is the intercept point for the line $y = 3x - 2$ and the line $y_1 = 2x + 4$?

    (A) $(2, 8)$
    (B) $(3, 7)$
    (C) $(6, 16)$
    (D) $(9, 22)$

37. Which of the following is perpendicular to the line $y = 2x + 4$?

(A) $y = -\dfrac{1}{2}x + 13$

(B) $y = \dfrac{1}{2}x + 5$

(C) $y = 2x + 6$

(D) $y = 4x + 4$

38. Which of the following lines is perpendicular to the line $y = \dfrac{1}{4}x + 3$ and passes through the point (2, 5)?

(A) $y = -4x + 13$

(B) $y = -4x + 5$

(C) $y = -\dfrac{1}{4}x + 4$

(D) $y = 4x + 13$

39. The line $y = mx$ passes through the point (2, 8). What is the value of m?

(A) -4

(B) $-\dfrac{1}{4}$

(C) $\dfrac{1}{4}$

(D) 4

40. Line ℓ has a negative slope, a positive y-intercept, and a positive x-intercept. If line m is parallel to line ℓ, which of the following statements must be true?

  I. Line m has a negative slope

  II. Line m has a positive y-intercept

  III. Line m has a positive x-intercept

(A) I only

(B) II only

(C) III only

(D) None of these statements must be true.

41. The line $y = -4x - 9$ passes through point B on the y-axis. What is the value of B?

(A) -15
(B) -9
(C) -5
(D) -4

42. The following table shows selected values on a line $y = mx + b$. What is the value of w?

x	-1	0	1
y	2	w	6

(A) -3
(B) 3
(C) 4
(D) 5

43. A person can get from Chuck's house to Carly's house by walking three blocks north, two blocks east, and then two more blocks north. In terms of blocks, what is the straight-line distance between Chuck's house and Carly's house?

(A) $3\sqrt{2}$

(B) $\sqrt{7}$

(C) $\sqrt{10}$

(D) $\sqrt{29}$

44. A line segment with a slope of -3 starts at the point $(0, 6)$ and ends at the point $(x, 0)$. What is the value of x?

(A) 1
(B) 2
(C) 3
(D) 6

45. A data-entry specialist started his day by typing 35 words per minute, steadily, for 4 hours, followed by a 1-hour break. Following his break, he steadily typed 20 words per minute for another 4 hours. Which of the following graphs best represents his total words typed (w) in terms of hours (h)?

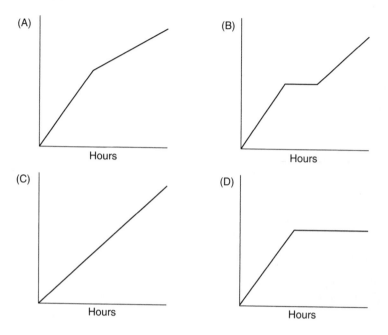

(A)

Hours

(B)

Hours

(C)

Hours

(D)

Hours

46. The line $y = 2x + 4$ passes through point A on the x-axis. Which of the following indicates the correct coordinates for that point?

(A) $(-2, 0)$
(B) $(0, -2)$
(C) $(0, 2)$
(D) $(2, 0)$

47. In the figure shown, B is the midpoint of AC. What is the value of x?

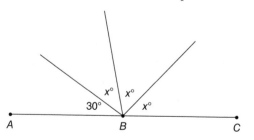

48. A line passes through the points $(t, t+4)$ and $(t+7, t+9)$. Which of the following represents the slope of the line?

(A) $-\dfrac{4}{9}$

(B) $\dfrac{7}{13}$

(C) $\dfrac{5}{7}$

(D) $\dfrac{2t+7}{2t+13}$

49. Which of the following lines is parallel?

   I. $y = 2x + 1$ and $y = 2x + 12$
   II. $y = -3x + 1$ and $y = 3x + 1$
   III. $y = \dfrac{1}{3}x + 4$ and $y = -3x + 2$

(A) I only
(B) I and II
(C) II and III
(D) III only

50. Two lines, line 1 and line 2, are perpendicular. If the slope of line 1 is a and the slope of line 2 is b, which of the following is equal to the product of a and b?

(A) -1
(B) 1
(C) a^2
(D) $\dfrac{1}{ab}$

51. The line $f(x) = tx + 1_1$. A second line can be defined as $g(x) = x - 3$. The intercept point is $(-4, -7)$. What is the correct value of t?

(A) $\dfrac{1}{2}$
(B) 1
(C) 2
(D) 3

52. Which of the following lines passes through the point $(0, 5)$?

(A) $f(x) = -3x + 5$
(B) $f(x) = -x + 4$
(C) $f(x) = 2x - 5$
(D) $f(x) = 5x + 3$

53. What are the coordinates of the point $(-1, 5)$ when it is reflected across the line $y = x$?

(A) $(-1, -5)$
(B) $(-5, -1)$
(C) $(5, -1)$
(D) $(1, 5)$

54. What is the slope of a line that passes through the points (x, y) and $(2x, 2y)$ where x and y are nonzero?

(A) $\dfrac{x}{y}$

(B) $\dfrac{y}{x}$

(C) $x - y$

(D) $y - x$

Questions 55–165 may be answered using a calculator. Remember, the calculator is a useful tool but may not be the most efficient method for solving every problem.

55. Let x and y be nonzero real numbers. If $2xy = 7(m + n)$ and $2(m + n) = 8$, what is the value of x in terms of y?

(A) $\dfrac{14}{y}$

(B) $\dfrac{8}{y}$

(C) $\dfrac{8}{7y}$

(D) $\dfrac{13}{2y}$

56. Which of the following represents the solution set of $-3x + 2 < -2x + 4$?

    (A) $x > 2$

    (B) $x > -2$

    (C) $-2 < x < -\dfrac{6}{5}$

    (D) $x > -\dfrac{6}{5}$

57. The chess club decides to sell T-shirts to raise money for an upcoming tournament. On the first day, they sell 14 large T-shirts and 10 small T-shirts, raising a total of $248. On the second day, they sell only 6 large and 2 small T-shirts, raising an additional $88. How much did the club charge for the small T-shirts?

    (A) $4

    (B) $6

    (C) $8

    (D) $10

58. If $x > 0$, $y > 0$, $x^2 = 9$, and $xy = 12$, then $(x - 2y)^2 =$

    (A) -30

    (B) -23

    (C) 17

    (D) 25

59. The value of an integer m is three times the value of an integer n, while the value of an integer k is twice the value of n. What is the value of k in terms of m?

    (A) $\dfrac{1}{3}m$

    (B) $\dfrac{2}{3}m$

    (C) $51m$

    (D) $6m$

60. If $(a - b)(b + a) = 6$ and $a^2 = 8$, what is the value of b^2?

61. Suppose p, q, r, and s are nonzero real numbers. If $pq = r$ and $q = \dfrac{s}{p}$, which of the following is equivalent to r?

    (A) 1

    (B) s

    (C) $p^2 s$

    (D) $\dfrac{p}{s}$

62. The value of $\dfrac{a}{b}$ is 6. What is the value of $\dfrac{2a}{3b}$?

    (A) 2
    (B) 4
    (C) 12
    (D) 18

63. If $\dfrac{\sqrt{x}}{4} = 8$, then what is $\dfrac{7\sqrt{x}}{4}$?

64. The value of an integer is one-eighth the value of another integer. If both integers are larger than 1, what is the smallest possible value of the smaller integer?

65. Which of the following is 8 more than $\dfrac{x+1}{y}$ for nonzero values of x and y?

    (A) $\dfrac{x+9}{y}$

    (B) $\dfrac{9x+1}{y}$

    (C) $\dfrac{x+1}{y+8}$

    (D) $\dfrac{x+8y+1}{y}$

66. If a is any positive integer, how many solutions to $-2 < x + 5 < 9$ can be written in the form $3a$?

    (A) One
    (B) Two
    (C) Three
    (D) Four

67. Which of the following represents the product of two consecutive odd integers m and n when $m < n$?

    (A) $m^2 + 1$
    (B) $m^2 + m$
    (C) $m^2 + 2m$
    (D) $m^2 + 2m + 1$

68. If a is 10 more than b and b is 7 less than c, which of the following represents the value of a in terms of c?

    (A) $c - 7$
    (B) $c - 3$
    (C) $c + 3$
    (D) $c + 7$

69. If $x - 4y = 15$ and $2x + 6y = 16$, what is the value of x?

70. The square of a nonzero number is equal to one-half that number. What is the value of the number?

71. A large recipe requires $20\frac{1}{2}$ pounds of flour. If flour can only be purchased in 50-pound bags, how many bags of flour must be purchased to make the recipe eight times?
(A) 2
(B) 3
(C) 4
(D) 5

72. Given that the square root of the sum of m and n is equal to the product of 4 and m, which of the following is equivalent to $m + n$?
(A) $4m$
(B) $16m^2$
(C) $4m - n^2$
(D) $16(m^2 - n^2)$

73. A company designs a box that can store c specialty game pieces for its latest board game. If five such game pieces are stored in the box, which of the following represents the number of pieces that can still be stored in the box?
(A) $c - 5$
(B) $c = 5$
(C) $5c$
(D) $\dfrac{c}{5}$

74. If $2xy = 26$ and $0 < x < 4$, which of the following is *not* a possible value of y?
(A) 3
(B) 5
(C) 8
(D) 12

75. If $-9x \le -28$, what is the smallest possible integer value of x?

76. If $\dfrac{1}{4} = \dfrac{3}{a} + \dfrac{1}{7}$, what is the value of a?

77. A number m is two-times as large as a number n. If n is 5 more than 8, what is the value of m?

78. If $\frac{1}{2}x = \frac{1}{4}y$, what is $\frac{3}{4}x + 1$ in terms of y?

   (A) $3y + 1$

   (B) $\frac{1}{2}y + 1$

   (C) $\frac{3}{8}y + 1$

   (D) $\frac{1}{2}y + \frac{1}{2}$

79. Let $m \Theta n = 3m^2 - n$. If $2 \Theta n = 9$, what is the value of n?
   (A) -12
   (B) -3
   (C) 3
   (D) 12

80. If $x - 2y = 8$, what is the value of $\frac{x}{2} - y$?
   (A) 2
   (B) 4
   (C) 10
   (D) 12

81. For all values of α, how much larger is $6\alpha + 5$ than $6\alpha - 3$?
   (A) 2
   (B) 3
   (C) 5
   (D) 8

82. If x is a solution to $3 < 2m + 1 < 10$, then which of the following *cannot* be a solution to the inequality?
   I. $\frac{1}{2}x$
   II. $2x$
   III. $5x$
   (A) I only
   (B) II only
   (C) III only
   (D) I and II only

83. An urn contains six more green marbles than it contains red marbles. If the number of red marbles is represented by r, which of the following expressions represents the total number of marbles in the urn?

    (A) $6r$
    (B) $r + 6$
    (C) $2r + 6$
    (D) $2r + 12$

84. If $x - 2 = 4x - 6$, what is the value of x?

85. If $4p + q = k$ and $p = 2q$, then in terms of p and q, k also equals which of the following?

    (A) $3q$
    (B) $9q$
    (C) $8p + q$
    (D) $8p + 2q$

86. Which of the following is half as large as $\dfrac{3x}{y} + \dfrac{1}{6}$ for all nonzero values of x and y?

    (A) $\dfrac{6x + y}{4y}$

    (B) $\dfrac{3x + y}{12y}$

    (C) $\dfrac{18x + y}{6y}$

    (D) $\dfrac{18x + y}{12y}$

87. A student can run 5 miles in 36 minutes. If the student maintains the same speed, how many miles can she run in 45 minutes?

    (A) $\dfrac{5}{36}$

    (B) $\dfrac{5}{4}$

    (C) $\dfrac{10}{4}$

    (D) $\dfrac{25}{4}$

88. If $2ab - a = 5$, then what is the value of $4ab - 2a + 4$?

89. How many positive integers are in the solution set of $3x < \dfrac{11}{2}$ and $-2 < x + 1 < 4$?

(A) None
(B) One
(C) Two
(D) Three

90. For what nonzero values of m and n is the inequality $(m + n)^2 \le (m - n)^2$ true?

(A) When $m > 0$ and $n > 0$
(B) When $m < 0$ and $n < 0$
(C) When m and n have opposite signs
(D) When m is twice as large as n

91. If $\sqrt{x - 1} = \dfrac{1}{4}$, then what does x equal?

92. If $a = 4b$ and $a > 14$, then which of the following must be true?

(A) $b > \dfrac{7}{2}$

(B) $b > \dfrac{5}{2}$

(C) $b > 4$
(D) $b > 10$

93. If $3m - n = 10$ and $-2m + 4n = 8$, what is the value of $m + 3n$?

(A) $\dfrac{24}{5}$

(B) $\dfrac{39}{5}$

(C) 10
(D) 18

94. Given that two-thirds of x is equivalent to the product of 5 and y, which of the following is equivalent to $15y$?

    (A) $\dfrac{2}{9}x$

    (B) $\dfrac{1}{3}x$

    (C) $\dfrac{5}{3}x$

    (D) $2x$

95. A single performance of a magic show requires the use of x envelopes, and the envelopes cannot be reused after a performance. Suppose the magician must perform his magic show y times this week. Which of the following expressions represents the number of envelopes he will need this week?

    (A) $\dfrac{x}{y}$

    (B) $\dfrac{y}{x}$

    (C) xy
    (D) $x + y$

96. What is the equation of the line whose graph is perpendicular to the graph of the line $y = -\dfrac{2}{3}x + \dfrac{1}{5}$ and passes through the point $\left(0, \dfrac{1}{8}\right)$?

    (A) $y = -\dfrac{2}{3}x + \dfrac{1}{8}$

    (B) $y = -\dfrac{2}{3}x - 8$

    (C) $y = \dfrac{3}{2}x + \dfrac{1}{8}$

    (D) $y = \dfrac{3}{2}x - 8$

97. In the figure shown, point R is the midpoint of $\overline{PQ}$, and $\overline{RS}$ has the same length as $\overline{PQ}$. If the length of $\overline{PQ}$ is 6, what is the length of $\overline{PS}$?

P   R   Q   S

(A) 3
(B) 6
(C) 9
(D) 12

98. The tick marks are equally spaced on the following graph. Which of the following line segments (not shown) would be parallel to $\overline{PQ}$?

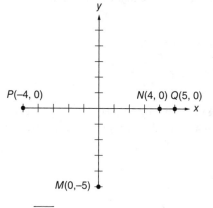

I. $\overline{QN}$

II. $\overline{MN}$

III. $\overline{PM}$

(A) I only
(B) II only
(C) III only
(D) I and II only

99. Two points lie on the coordinate grid: A (4, 6) and B (−2, 6). What point below is at the midpoint of line $\overline{AB}$?

(A) (1, 6)
(B) (2, 6)
(C) (6, 1)
(D) (6, 2)

100. Line ℓ passes through the point $(0, 4)$, and line m passes through the point $(2, 0)$. If the two lines are parallel and the slope of line ℓ is undefined, what is the shortest distance between a point on ℓ and a point on m?

(A) $\sqrt{2}$

(B) 2

(C) $2\sqrt{5}$

(D) $4\sqrt{5}$

101. The line ℓ is perpendicular to the line $3y + x = 4$ and passes through the point $(0, -5)$. The line $y = t$ intersects ℓ at the point $(-4, t)$. What is the value of t?

(A) -17

(B) -15

(C) -8

(D) -3

102. A right triangle is formed in the xy-plane by connecting the points $(1, 1)$, $(1, 4)$, and $(0, 1)$. What is the length of the hypotenuse of this triangle?

(A) $\sqrt{2}$

(B) $\sqrt{3}$

(C) $\sqrt{6}$

(D) $\sqrt{10}$

103. The slopes of two parallel lines are p and q, respectively. If the sum of p and q is $\dfrac{7}{8}$, what is the value of p?

104. In the figure shown, lines ℓ and m are perpendicular. If $2x = y$, what is the value of y in degrees?

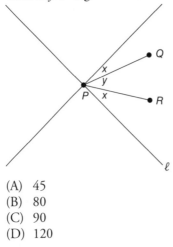

(A) 45

(B) 80

(C) 90

(D) 120

105. Two lines m and n are parallel and have positive slopes. If the product of the slopes is c, which of the following represents the slope of line m in terms of c?

(A) $\dfrac{c}{2}$

(B) $\sqrt{c}$

(C) $2c$

(D) c^2

106. In the following figure, lines m and n are parallel. If $p = 2q$, what is the value of z in terms of w in degrees?

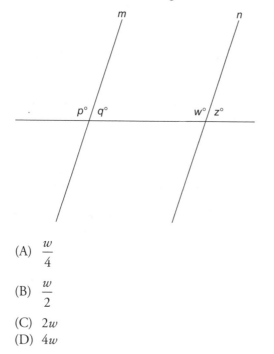

(A) $\dfrac{w}{4}$

(B) $\dfrac{w}{2}$

(C) $2w$

(D) $4w$

107. If the shortest distance from point $P\,(1,\,4)$ to the x-axis is m and the shortest distance from point P to the y-axis is n, what is the value of $m + n$?

(A) 1

(B) $\sqrt{2}$

(C) $\sqrt{3}$

(D) 5

108. If a line in the xy-plane has a slope of 1 and passes through the point $(1, 5)$, then each of the following points could be on the line *except*

(A) $(-10, -6)$
(B) $(-8, -3)$
(C) $(-2, 2)$
(D) $(2, 6)$

109. Line m is parallel to the x-axis and passes through the point $(5, 2)$. What is the y-intercept of m?

(A) -5
(B) -2
(C) 1
(D) 2

110. The points A, B, C, and D lie on a line in alphabetical order such that the length of $\overline{BC}$ is 4 and the length of $\overline{CD}$ is 10. If B is the midpoint of $\overline{AC}$, what is the length of $\overline{AD}$?

111. The slopes of two lines are m and n, respectively. If $m + n = 0$, which of the following statements must be true?

(A) The lines are parallel.
(B) The lines are perpendicular.
(C) The line with slope m is perpendicular to the line with slope n.
(D) The line with slope $-m$ is parallel to the line with slope n.

112. Given the y-coordinate of any point on line n, the x-coordinate can be found using the formula $x = -5y + 10$. What is the slope of line n?

(A) -2
(B) $-\dfrac{1}{5}$
(C) $-\dfrac{1}{10}$
(D) 2

113. The following table represents values of a linear function f for selected values of x. What is the value of a?

f	-1	1	3
x	6	2	a

(A) -6
(B) -2
(C) 1
(D) 3

114. Which of the following is the equation of a line that passes through the origin?

    (A) $y + 5x = -2$
    (B) $-3y - x = 1$
    (C) $2x + 2y = -1$
    (D) $3x - 4y = 0$

115. If the rectangle in the figure shown is reflected across the x-axis, what are the coordinates of point D?

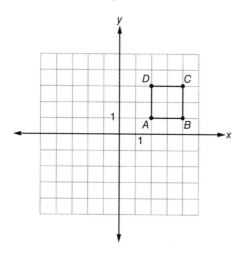

    (A) $(-2, -3)$
    (B) $(-2, 3)$
    (C) $(2, -3)$
    (D) $(2, 3)$

116. $P(-5, 0)$, $Q(0, 5)$, $R(5, 0)$, and $S(0, -5)$ are points on a coordinate grid. Which of the following line segments will have a slope of -1?

    (A) $\overline{PQ}$

    (B) $\overline{QR}$

    (C) $\overline{RS}$

    (D) $\overline{QS}$

117. A family taking a road trip by car travels at a constant speed with 1-hour breaks every 3 hours. Which of the following graphs could represent the total number of miles the family drives in 12 hours?

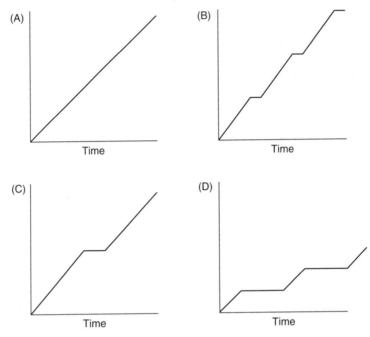

118. If the point $(-7, 19)$ is on a line m with an undefined slope, which of the following points would also be on line m?

    (A) $(-7, 0)$
    (B) $(0, 19)$
    (C) $(0, -7)$
    (D) $(19, 0)$

119. What is the area of a circle with a center at $(1, 3)$ and the point $(4, 6)$ on its circumference?

    (A) 3π
    (B) 6π
    (C) 9π
    (D) 18π

120. If the area of a circle is 9π, what is the circumference of the same circle?

    (A) 3π
    (B) 6π
    (C) $3\pi^2$
    (D) $9\pi^2$

121. If point P is on the x-axis and point Q is on the y-axis, what is the product of their x-coordinates?

(A) −2
(B) −1
(C) 0
(D) 1

122. Starting from point M, a plane flies due north for 1 hour, due west for 3 hours, and due north again for 2 hours to reach point N. The speed of the plane remains constant at 200 mph for the entire journey. If point M is labeled as the origin with north as the positive direction of the y-axis, what are the coordinates of point N?

(A) (1200, 0)
(B) (−600, 400)
(C) (600, 200)
(D) (−600, 600)

123. Two points (a, b) and (c, d) lie along the same line k in the xy-plane. If $a - c = 5$ and $b - d = 15$, what is the slope of the line?

(A) −3
(B) $-\dfrac{1}{3}$
(C) $\dfrac{1}{3}$
(D) 3

124. Points A, B, C, D, and E are arranged on a line in that order such that D is the midpoint of line segment $\overline{CE}$. If both $\overline{AB}$ and $\overline{CD}$ have a length of 3, then which of the following is a possible value for the length of line segment $\overline{AE}$?

(A) 5
(B) 6
(C) 7
(D) 12

125. In the following figure, the tick marks on the x- and y-axes are evenly spaced. If the slope of line segment PQ (not shown) is m, which of the following line segments has a slope of $\dfrac{m}{2}$?

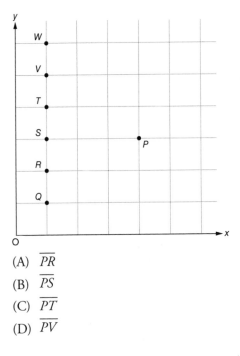

    (A) $\overline{PR}$
    (B) $\overline{PS}$
    (C) $\overline{PT}$
    (D) $\overline{PV}$

126. Two lines in the standard xy-plane are parallel. If the points $(-1, 4)$ and $(0, 5)$ are on one of the lines, which of the following could be a point on the other line?

    (A) $(-10, -5)$
    (B) $(-5, 0)$
    (C) $(-2, 6)$
    (D) $(3, 8)$

127. If the point $P\,(3, 9)$ is reflected across the line $y = x$, what are the new coordinates of P?

    (A) $(9, 3)$
    (B) $(9, 0)$
    (C) $(-3, -9)$
    (D) $(-9, -3)$

128. Circle A has a radius R. Circle B has a radius of $3R$. What is the ratio between the area of circle B to the area of circle A?

129. The slope of a line n that passes through the point $(-2, -1)$ is 2. Which of the following points is *not* on line n?

   (A) (0, 2)
   (B) (1, 5)
   (C) (3, 9)
   (D) (5, 13)

130. Circle A has a radius R, and circle B has a radius of $3R$. What is the ratio between the circumference of circle B to the diameter of circle A?

   (A) 3π
   (B) 3
   (C) 9π
   (D) 6

131. A line in the standard xy-plane passes through the points (8, 2) and $(-2, 6)$. Which of the following is the equation of a line perpendicular to this line?

   (A) $5y + 2x = 20$
   (B) $2y - 5x = -12$
   (C) $2y + 5x = 14$
   (D) $5y - 2x = -15$

132. Luisa is planning a bake sale. Each dozen (12) cupcakes will cost $3.25 in materials to bake, and Luisa plans to sell each cupcake for $1.50. Which expression represents Luisa's net profit in dollars after selling x dozen cupcakes?

   (A) $1.5x - 3.25x$
   (B) $1.5(12) - 3.25x$
   (C) $18x - 3.25x$
   (D) $18x - 3.25\left(\dfrac{x}{12}\right)$

133. If $-\dfrac{3}{8} \le \dfrac{m}{-2} + 8 \le 7$, which of the following values for m satisfy the inequality?

   (A) 0
   (B) 1
   (C) 2
   (D) 17

134. If $\dfrac{x}{2} = 2 + \dfrac{1}{2}y$ and $y - 8 = 24$, what is the value of $x^2 - y^2$?

(A) 272
(B) 136
(C) 144
(D) 16

135. If $\dfrac{2}{x} - 10 = 12$, what is the value of x?

136. If $3x = 8y - 3$ and $4y + 2x = 5$, what is the value of $\dfrac{x}{y}$?

(A) $\dfrac{3}{4}$

(B) $\dfrac{4}{3}$

(C) 3
(D) 5

137. Steve and Brian are taking a cross-country road trip. They have agreed to split the cost of gas evenly. The price of gas is \$4 per gallon. If the minivan, when traveling at a constant rate of 60 miles per hour (mph), is able to travel x miles on 1 gallon, which of the following expressions represents the dollar amount that each pays for a trip covering 150 miles when the minivan is traveling at a constant rate of 60 mph?

(A) $2\left(\dfrac{150}{x}\right)$

(B) $4\left(\dfrac{x}{150}\right)$

(C) $8\left(\dfrac{150}{x}\right)$

(D) $10\left(\dfrac{x}{150}\right)$

138. In the system of equations shown, what is the value of $x + y$?

$$2x - 1 = 4(y + 2)$$
$$x + 4y = 6$$

(A) $\dfrac{1}{4}$

(B) $\dfrac{19}{4}$

(C) $\dfrac{21}{4}$

(D) 5

139. Which of the following lines is not perpendicular to the line with equation $2y + 5x = -11$?

(A) $5y = 2x + \dfrac{3}{2}$

(B) $y = \dfrac{5}{2}x + 6$

(C) $10y - 5 = 4x$

(D) $-5y = -2x - 4$

140. Which of the following values of x does *not* satisfy this inequality: $-59 > -3x - 5 > -110$?

(A) 12

(B) 18

(C) 30

(D) 35

141. Based on the system of equations shown, what is the sum of a and b?

$$3a + 2b = 33$$
$$a - 5b = -2a - 9$$

(A) −1

(B) 5

(C) 7

(D) 13

142. The first term of a sequence is 2, and the remaining terms of the sequence are defined by the formula $a_n = 1 - a_{n-1}$, where a_n is the nth term of the sequence. What is the third term of the sequence?

    (A) −3
    (B) −2
    (C) −1
    (D) 2

143. The following pictogram shows the annual expenditure on park maintenance for a small town for three selected years. How much more was spent in 2000 than in 2010?

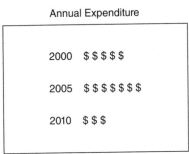

Annual Expenditure

    2000 $ $ $ $
    2005 $ $ $ $ $ $
    2010 $ $ $

$ = 25,000 Dollars

    (A) $3000
    (B) $5000
    (C) $50,000
    (D) $75,000

144. Let x represent 3.174 rounded to the nearest tenth, and let y represent 3.174 rounded to the nearest hundredth. What is the value of $x + y$?

145. The first term of a sequence is 4, and each subsequent term is determined by multiplying the previous term by the integer m. If the third term of the sequence is 16 and the sixth term of the sequence is −128, what is the value of m?

146. For integers m and n, define $m \Pi n = 2m - 4n$. What is the value of $3 \Pi (-2)$?

    (A) −16
    (B) −2
    (C) 4
    (D) 14

147. The values of $4a$ and $2b^{\frac{1}{2}}$ are the same. If a represents the smallest prime number, what is the value of b?

(A) 2
(B) 16
(C) 8
(D) 9

148. A firm suggests that its employees spend between 8 and 14 hours per week on each of their assigned cases. If h represents the number of hours, which of the following inequalities would best represent this suggestion?

(A) $|h - 3| < 11$
(B) $|h - 6| < 14$
(C) $|h - 6| < 8$
(D) $|h - 11| < 3$

149. Let x $(\therefore)$ y be defined as $3xy$ and ∂x as $5x - 1$ for integers x and y. Suppose $5x(\therefore)2 = 2y$ and $\partial x = 14$. What is the value of $3y$?

(A) 270
(B) 135
(C) 48
(D) 45

150. If $|4x - 9| = 19$ and x is a positive integer, what is the value of x?

(A) 2
(B) 6
(C) 7
(D) 10

151. Let x represent a real number that is a multiple of 6 and divisible by 14. If $x < 100$, what is the largest possible value of x?

152. If $\sqrt{n} > 5$ for a positive integer n, then for an integer $m > 1$, $\sqrt[m]{n}$ must be larger than which of the following?

(A) 5
(B) $5\sqrt{n}$
(C) $\sqrt[m]{5}$
(D) $\sqrt[m]{5n}$

153. The nth term of a sequence a_n is defined by the formula $a_n = \dfrac{a_{n-1}}{2}$. If the fifth term of the sequence is 10, what is the first term of the sequence?

(A) $\dfrac{1}{32}$

(B) $\dfrac{1}{10}$

(C) 20

(D) 160

154. If $x - 5 > 7$, which of the following is a possible value of x?

(A) -12
(B) -10
(C) 0
(D) 15

155. If $(xy)^2 = 36$, each of the following is a possible value of $x + y$ *except*

(A) -5
(B) -1
(C) 5
(D) $\dfrac{25}{2}$

156. What is the next term in the geometric sequence $16, -4, 1, -\dfrac{1}{4} \ldots$?

(A) $-\dfrac{1}{8}$

(B) 0

(C) $\dfrac{1}{16}$

(D) $\dfrac{1}{2}$

157. A dairy company processes raw milk. The number of gallons of milk the company can produce during t days using Process A is $A(t) = t^2 + 2t$. Using Process B, the number of gallons of milk produced during t days is $B(t) = 10t$. The company has only 7 days to produce milk and must choose one of the processes. What is the maximum amount of milk produced, in gallons, for this period?

(A) 8
(B) 10
(C) 31
(D) 70

158. Suppose a is a positive integer such that $b = \dfrac{3}{|-a|}$. Which of the following is a possible value of b?

(A) $-\dfrac{3}{16}$

(B) $\dfrac{3}{5}$

(C) 2

(D) 11

159. For what value of k will the two equations $2x + 4 = 4(x - 2)$ and $-x + k = 2x - 1$ have the same solution?

(A) 6
(B) 2
(C) 17
(D) –1

160. a, b, c, and d are numbers of different values such that $a + b = d$ and $a * b * c = 0$. Which of the 4 numbers *must* be equal to 0?

(A) a
(B) b
(C) c
(D) d

161. If a and b are both even numbers, which of the following could be an odd number?

(A) $a^2 + b^2$
(B) $(a + 1)^2 + (b + 1)^2$
(C) $(a + 1) * (b + 1)^2$
(D) $a + b$

162. If x is a negative number, which of the following *must* be true?

I. $x^5 < |x|$

II. $x < \sqrt{(-x)}$

III. $\dfrac{x - 1}{|x|} < 0$

(A) I, II and III
(B) I and II only
(C) None
(D) II and III only

163. Line ℓ passes through the points $(-2, 0)$ and $(0, a)$. Line j passes through the points $(4, 0)$ and $(6, 2)$. What value of a makes the two lines parallel?

(A) 1/2

(B) −2

(C) 2

(D) −1/2

164. Let a, b, and c represent real numbers such that $a < 0 < b < c$. Which of the following inequalities must also be true?

I. $a^2 < b^2 < c^2$

II. $c - b > a$

III. $c + a > b$

(A) I only

(B) II only

(C) III only

(D) I and III only

165. Suppose for real numbers m and n, $m^2 < m$ and $n > 0$. Which of the following inequalities must be true?

(A) $mn < 0$

(B) $\dfrac{n}{m} > n$

(C) $mn > n$

(D) $n^2 > m^2$

Problem Solving and Data Analysis

Problem Solving and Data Analysis comprises approximately one-third of the SAT Math test. The questions involve interpreting data, applying real-world data analysis, and using visual aids to organize or analyze information.

Topics

- Averages: mean, median, mode
- Ratios, proportions, and rates
- Percents
- Probabilities
- Linear and exponential growth
- Table data, graphs, and scatterplots

Skills

- Solve word problems to calculate ratios, rates, percentages, and proportions
- Use ratios, rates, percentages, and proportions to solve problems
- Use table data to interpret data and solve problems
- Evaluate table data, graphs, and scatterplots to determine proportions and density or for accuracy
- Use statistics to determine mean, median, and mode

Need to Know

- Average is the same as mean.
- Mean = sum of total terms divided by number of different terms.
- Probability = number of desired outcomes divided by total number of possible outcomes.
- To determine the percent of a number n use $n\left(\dfrac{x}{100}\right)$.

- To determine what percent a number n is of another number m use $\dfrac{(n100)}{m}$.

- To determine what number n is x percent of use $\dfrac{(n100)}{x}$.

Questions 166–212 should be answered without a calculator.

166. A set of integers contains all integers greater than 1 and less than 15. If an integer is randomly selected from this set, what is the probability it is smaller than 5?

   (A) $\dfrac{1}{13}$

   (B) $\dfrac{3}{13}$

   (C) $\dfrac{5}{13}$

   (D) $\dfrac{9}{13}$

167. A data set contains eight numbers. If the mean of this data set is 4, what is the sum of the numbers in the data set?

   (A) 8
   (B) 16
   (C) 32
   (D) 64

168. A jar contains twice as many red coins as it does blue coins. If a coin is selected at random, what is the probability the coin is blue?

   (A) $\dfrac{1}{5}$

   (B) $\dfrac{1}{4}$

   (C) $\dfrac{1}{3}$

   (D) $\dfrac{1}{2}$

169. The area of one circle is half the area of another circle. If the radius of the larger circle is r, which of the following expressions represents the average area of the two circles?

(A) $2\pi r$

(B) πr^2

(C) $\dfrac{\pi}{2} r^2$

(D) $\dfrac{3\pi}{4} r^2$

170. The numbers n_1, n_2, n_3, n_4, n_5 are consecutive integers, and the median of the list is 3. What is the median of the list $n_1 + 5, n_2 + 5, n_3 + 5, n_4 + 5, n_5 + 5$?

(A) 6

(B) 7

(C) 8

(D) 9

171. The median of a list of 10 integers is 14. When the integers are placed in order from smallest to largest, the fifth integer in the list is 11. What is the value of the sixth integer in the list?

172. In a line to claim a prize, Jackie is both twelfth counting from the front of the line and twelfth counting from the back of the line. How many people are in line to claim the prize?

(A) 20

(B) 22

(C) 23

(D) 24

173. The management of a theater sent out surveys to determine how many plays its previous patrons had attended in the last year. The results are shown in the following table. What is the median number of plays attended by all the patrons of this theater?

Number of Plays Attended	Number of Patrons
2	25
3	15
4	35
5	10
6	5
7	2

174. Matt is a college student who spends 6 hours per day studying, 3 hours exercising for the college football team, and approximately 3 hours reading. He spends 9 hours sleeping. What is the probability of selecting a random time when Matt is not sleeping during any given day?

    (A) $\dfrac{1}{8}$

    (B) $\dfrac{1}{4}$

    (C) $\dfrac{3}{8}$

    (D) $\dfrac{2}{3}$

175. In a certain game, points are awarded based on which integer is randomly selected from the integers 1, 2, 3, 4, 5, 6, 7, 8, 9, 10. If an even integer is selected, 5 points are awarded. Otherwise, 2 points are awarded. If the game is played once, what is the probability the player will earn 2 points?

176. Joseph spends his time at school attending classes, practicing football, and completing homework assignments. Typically, he will spend 7 hours in classes, 2 hours in football practice, and 1 hour completing homework. If a randomly selected time is chosen during a typical school day, what is the probability Joseph is *not* in a class?

    (A) $\dfrac{1}{10}$

    (B) $\dfrac{3}{10}$

    (C) $\dfrac{2}{7}$

    (D) $\dfrac{3}{7}$

177. Jane is going to the theater. The theater tickets are numbered from 1 to 20. What is the probability that her ticket will be a multiple of either 3 or 7?

    (A) $\dfrac{3}{20}$

    (B) $\dfrac{1}{4}$

    (C) $\dfrac{2}{5}$

    (D) $\dfrac{1}{2}$

178. One card is drawn from a pack that has 52 cards. What is the probability of that card being a jack, queen, or king?

(A) $\dfrac{3}{52}$

(B) $\dfrac{3}{13}$

(C) $\dfrac{7}{26}$

(D) $\dfrac{31}{52}$

179. The following picture represents the total monthly attendance to a live music venue's concerts for three selected months. How many more people attended the venue's concerts in May than in January?

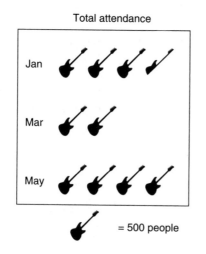

Total attendance

= 500 people

(A) 250
(B) 500
(C) 1750
(D) 2000

180. Out of nine members, a club must select three officers, each with a different rank. A club member may not be selected as an officer more than once. How many different ways can the three officers be selected?

(A) 9
(B) 27
(C) 504
(D) 729

181. The median of five positive integers is 15. What is the smallest possible value of any of these integers?

182. An ice cream shop offers m types of ice cream, n types of syrup, and p types of toppings. How many different orders including one flavor of ice cream, one flavor of syrup, and one topping are possible?

    (A) mnp
    (B) $m + n + p$
    (C) $m - n - p$
    (D) $m^3 n^2 p$

183. A club with 20 members must select 2 who will act as ushers at an upcoming event. How many ways can the 2 ushers be selected?

    (A) 260
    (B) 380
    (C) 400
    (D) 420

184. In a single roll of a fair six-sided die, what is the probability a 3 comes up?

185. Two symbols from the set $\{\varepsilon, \phi, \Delta, \Omega, \forall, \Pi\}$ are to be selected as part of generating a random password. Any symbol that is selected can be selected again. In how many ways can the two symbols be selected?

    (A) 2
    (B) 12
    (C) 30
    (D) 36

186. In the scatterplot shown, which of the following is the x-coordinate of the point that is farthest from the line of best fit?

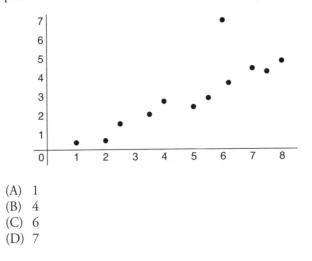

    (A) 1
    (B) 4
    (C) 6
    (D) 7

187. In a list of eight numbers, each value is 10 more than the previous value. If the smallest value in the list is 15, what is the median of the list?

(A) 40
(B) 45
(C) 50
(D) 55

188. A vehicle travels at a constant speed of m miles per hour. Which of the following represents the distance the vehicle will cover in 15 minutes in terms of m?

(A) $\dfrac{m}{4}$

(B) $\dfrac{m}{2}$

(C) $4m$
(D) $2m$

189. Rectangles A and B are similar such that the length of A is 5 and the length of B is 25. If the width of A is w, which of the following represents the width of B in terms of w?

(A) $\dfrac{w}{5}$

(B) $w - 5$
(C) $w + 5$
(D) $5w$

190. Suppose y varies directly as x and $y = c^3$ when $x = c^2$ for some nonzero constant c. What is the value of y when $x = 5$?

(A) $\dfrac{c^2}{10}$

(B) $\dfrac{c}{5}$

(C) $5c$
(D) $10c$

191. There are different letters labeled A, B, C, and D in a bag. The ratio of these letters is 4:3:7:2. There are 60 more A letters than D letters. What is the total number of B letters?

(A) 15
(B) 30
(C) 45
(D) 60

192. Suppose m varies inversely as n. If when $m = 5$, $n = 1$, then when $n = x$, $m =$

(A) $5x$

(B) $\dfrac{1}{5x}$

(C) $\dfrac{5}{x}$

(D) $\dfrac{x}{5}$

193. A recipe requires that the amount of flour and sugar used follow a ratio of 2:3. If $1\dfrac{1}{4}$ cups of flour are used, how many cups of sugar should be used?

194. The figure shown indicates the total number of customer service calls completed (in hundreds) by a group of customer service agents at the same company as measured over a 4-week period. According to the chart, between which two consecutive weeks was there the greatest increase in the number of customer service calls completed?

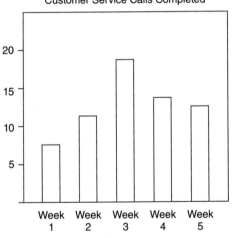

Customer Service Calls Completed

(A) Week 1 and week 2
(B) Week 2 and week 3
(C) Week 3 and week 4
(D) This cannot be determined from the information given.

195. The bar graph shown represents the percentage of movies owned by a particular family. Which of the following pie charts best represents the information provided?

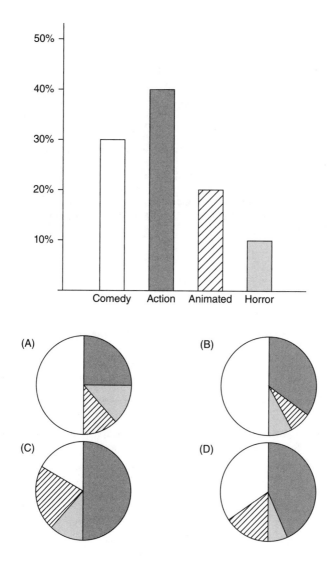

196. If a is directly proportional to b and $a = 18$ when $b = 3$, then what is a when $b = \dfrac{1}{3}$?

(A) $\dfrac{1}{18}$

(B) $\dfrac{46}{3}$

(C) 2

(D) 15

197. The length of a sailboat is 60 feet. If a scale model of this boat is to be built such that the ratio of the model to the actual sailboat is 1:80, what will the length of the model be in feet?

198. The ratio of the height of triangle A to the height of triangle B is 1:3. If the triangles are similar, what is the ratio of the area of triangle A to the area of triangle B?

(A) 1:3

(B) 1:6

(C) 1:9

(D) 1:12

199. If the ratio of x to y is 2:7, which of the following equations must be true?

(A) $x - y = 5$

(B) $xy = 14$

(C) $2x = 7y$

(D) $7x = 2y$

200. If a hand sanitizer bottle containing 60 ml has 15% alcohol, how many ml of water should be added for the hand sanitizer to have only 10% alcohol?

(A) 9

(B) 15

(C) 30

(D) 45

201. If 80% of x is 480, then what does x equal?

202. The scatter plot shows the ranking of 10 students in two sports. How many students received the same rank in both the sports?

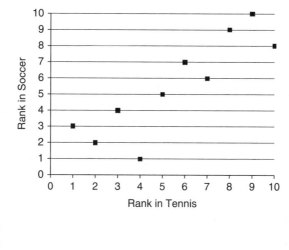

(A) 2
(B) 5
(C) 4
(D) 1

203. Gina rides her bike to the grocery store from her house at an average speed of 12 miles per hour and returns along the same route at an average speed of 18 miles per hour. If her total travel time was 45 minutes, what is the total round-trip distance, in miles, from her house to the grocery store and back?

204. A restaurant stocks dinner and dessert plates in a ratio of 5:3. If the restaurant stocks a total of n plates for dinner and dessert, which of the following represents the number of dinner plates?

(A) $\dfrac{5n}{8}$

(B) $\dfrac{5n}{3}$

(C) $2n$
(D) $3n$

205. If x is a positive number, what percentage of $5x$ is x?

(A) 2%
(B) 5%
(C) 20%
(D) 50%

206. In dollars, which of the following represents the price of an $\$m$ item after a 10% discount?

(A) $\dfrac{1}{10}m$

(B) $\dfrac{1}{5}m$

(C) $\dfrac{4}{5}m$

(D) $\dfrac{9}{10}m$

207. If x and y are positive numbers, which of the following is equivalent to $\dfrac{1}{x}\%$ of $\dfrac{25}{y}$?

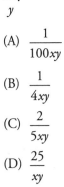

(A) $\dfrac{1}{100xy}$

(B) $\dfrac{1}{4xy}$

(C) $\dfrac{2}{5xy}$

(D) $\dfrac{25}{xy}$

208. If 0.06% of x is 6, then $x =$

(A) 10

(B) 100

(C) 1000

(D) 10,000

209. A factory is able to produce two large machines every 3 days. How many complete machines can be completed by the factory in 20 days?

(A) 6

(B) 7

(C) 12

(D) 13

210. If 15% of a number is 35, then 3% of the number is

(A) 4

(B) 5

(C) 6

(D) 7

211. The ratio of the numbers x, y, and z is 1:3:5. If $y = x + 1$, what is the value of z?

212. The chart shown indicates the total sales in thousands of dollars for two different locations of a pizza restaurant. According to the chart, which of the following is the closest to the total sales in July and August at the Jefferson City location?

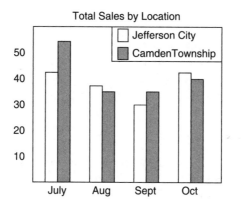

Total Sales by Location

(A) $73,000
(B) $79,000
(C) $85,000
(D) $89,000

213. What is the arithmetic mean of the numbers $5x$, $3x$, $2x$, and $8x$?

(A) $\dfrac{9x}{2}$

(B) $9x$

(C) $12x$

(D) $18x$

Calculator Questions 214–310

214. The probability of event A occurring is 0.25, and the probability of event B occurring is 0.30. If the two events are independent, what is the probability of both events occurring?

(A) 0.075
(B) 0.150
(C) 0.550
(D) 0.850

215. In a group of 80 people, the probability of selecting someone who is older than 25 is $\frac{3}{4}$. How many people in the group are 25 years old or younger?

216. What is the median of the following set of numbers 12, 6, 1, 1, 4?

(A) 1
(B) 3
(C) 4
(D) 5

217. How many passwords consisting of four digits between 0 and 9 inclusive are made up of all odd numbers?

(A) 4
(B) 16
(C) 24
(D) 625

218. Gregory has 15 different science fiction books and will randomly select four of these books to donate to charity. How many different possible ways can he select the four books?

(A) 19
(B) 60
(C) 974
(D) 32,760

219. The average of p, q, and r is 12. When the number m is included in the list, the average increases to 20. What is the value of m?

(A) 8
(B) 32
(C) 44
(D) 65

220. The students in a classroom are either seniors or juniors, and exactly 15 of the students are seniors. If the probability of randomly selecting a senior from this classroom is $\frac{5}{9}$, how many students in the classroom are juniors?

(A) 5
(B) 12
(C) 15
(D) 27

221. The numbers in the set {1, 4, 6, 8} are arranged into a four-digit number. If the number created is always less than 2000, how many different arrangements are possible?

222. What is the average (arithmetic mean) of $2x$, $x + 4$, and 5?

    (A) $x + 3$
    (B) $x + 9$
    (C) $3x + 3$
    (D) $3x + 4$

223. The special at a restaurant consists of a choice of one appetizer, one entrée, and one dessert. There are twice as many choices for an appetizer as there are for entrées, and there are five more dessert choices than appetizer choices. If there are four choices for an appetizer, how many different possible specials can be ordered?

224. The average of three consecutive integers is 150. What is the median of these three integers?

225. In a group of people, 150 of the people are younger than 38 years old, while 29 of the people are 38 years old or older. Which of the following must be true about the median age of people in this group?

    (A) The median age is less than 38.
    (B) The median age is 38.
    (C) The median age is between 29 and 38.
    (D) The median age may be less or more than 38.

226. If 75% of the students in a class had an average test score of 82, while the remaining students in the class had an average test score of 79, what was the average test score for the entire class?

    (A) 40.13
    (B) 79.25
    (C) 80.25
    (D) 81.25

227. In the following figure, there are three paths from A to B and four paths from B to C between the indicated points. How many different paths are possible from A to C?

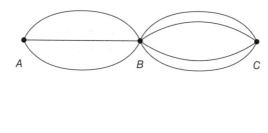

    (A) 6
    (B) 9
    (C) 12
    (D) 16

228. What is the probability a randomly generated two-digit number is less than 15?

229. What is the average (arithmetic mean) of $2x^2$ and $4x$?

    (A) $3x^2$

    (B) $x^2 + 2x$

    (C) $x^2 + 4x$

    (D) $2x^2 + 4x + 2$

230. Two triangles share the same length base, but the height of one triangle is three times the height of the other. If the average area of the two triangles is 10, what is the area of the smaller triangle?

    (A) $\dfrac{5}{2}$

    (B) 5

    (C) $\dfrac{20}{3}$

    (D) 10

231. If the following steps are completed once, what is the probability the resulting remainder will be zero?

Step 1 Randomly select a number from the set $\{4, 6, 7, 14, 18, 21\}$.
Step 2 Subtract 2 from the selected number.
Step 3 Divide the number by 4 and determine the remainder.

    (A) $\dfrac{1}{6}$

    (B) $\dfrac{1}{3}$

    (C) $\dfrac{1}{2}$

    (D) $\dfrac{2}{3}$

232. Half of the construction paper in a classroom is blue, while the other half is orange. A teacher brings in a new box of blue construction paper, bringing the total number of boxes of blue paper to five. What is the probability a randomly selected box of paper is orange?

    (A) $\dfrac{1}{5}$

    (B) $\dfrac{1}{2}$

    (C) $\dfrac{4}{9}$

    (D) $\dfrac{5}{9}$

233. If the median of x, $-2x$, and x^2 is x, which of the following can be a value of x?

(A) 2
(B) 1/2
(C) –1
(D) –2

234. In how many ways can four of five different paintings be displayed in a row on a wall?

235. If $0 < x < 1$, what is the median of $3x$, x, x^3, x^2, and x^4?

(A) $3x$
(B) x
(C) x^3
(D) x^2

236. The following figure represents a circle with center O that is divided into three segments: A, B, and C. If a point within the circle is randomly selected, what is the probability it will be in segment B?

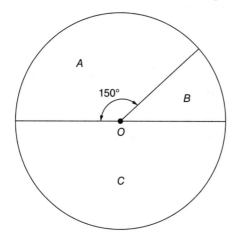

(A) $\dfrac{1}{12}$

(B) $\dfrac{1}{9}$

(C) $\dfrac{1}{4}$

(D) $\dfrac{1}{3}$

237. The median time for six students to finish an exam was 1 hour 25 minutes. In minutes, which of the following is the sum of the third- and fourth-fastest times?

(A) 70
(B) 85
(C) 170
(D) 255

238. A set contains 10 identical numbers. If that number is represented by n, which of the following statements must be true?

   I. The average of the 10 numbers is n.
   II. The median of the 10 numbers is n.
   III. The median of the 10 numbers is $\frac{n}{2}$.

(A) I only
(B) II only
(C) III only
(D) I and II

239. The mean of a set of 15 unique numbers is 135. If the five largest numbers are removed from the set, which of the following statements must be true about the new set?

(A) The mean will be 130.
(B) The mean will remain 135.
(C) The mean will be smaller than 135, but it may or may not be 130.
(D) The mean will no longer be 135, but it may be smaller or larger than 135.

240. The mean of the data set $\left\{x_1, x_2, x_3, x_4, y_1, y_2, y_3\right\}$ is 6. If the mean of the set $\left\{x_1, x_2, x_3, x_4\right\}$ is 3, what is the mean of the set $\{y_1, y_2, y_3\}$?

(A) 4
(B) 9
(C) 10
(D) 12

241. There were 225 people surveyed about what type of television service they use. Of these, 183 people use cable and 42 use satellite dish. Which equation would you use to estimate how many people would have cable if 600 people were surveyed?

(A) $\dfrac{225}{183} = \dfrac{x}{600}$

(B) $\dfrac{x}{600} = \dfrac{183}{225}$

(C) $600 = x * \dfrac{183}{225}$

(D) $\dfrac{225}{600} = \dfrac{x}{183}$

242. The probability of event A occurring is $\dfrac{x}{4}$, while the probability of event B occurring is $\dfrac{3x}{8}$. If the two events cannot occur at the same time, what is the probability event A or event B will occur?

(A) $\dfrac{x}{8}$

(B) $\dfrac{x}{3}$

(C) $\dfrac{5x}{8}$

(D) $\dfrac{3x^2}{32}$

243. If $y = 8$, what is the numerical value of the median of $3y$, $\dfrac{2}{3}y$, $10y$, and $\dfrac{7}{3}y$?

244. Based on the graph, estimate how many students participated in viewing activities in a campus with 1400 students.

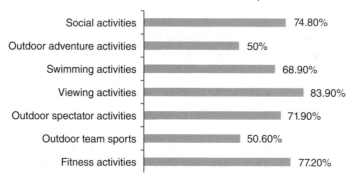

Outdoor Activities on Campus

Activity	Percentage
Social activities	74.80%
Outdoor adventure activities	50%
Swimming activities	68.90%
Viewing activities	83.90%
Outdoor spectator activities	71.90%
Outdoor team sports	50.60%
Fitness activities	77.20%

245. A data set consists of the number 1 n times and the number 3 one time. If $n > 1$, which of the following statements must be true about the mean and the median?

(A) The mean and the median will equal 1.
(B) The mean will be larger than 1, and the median will be equal to 1.
(C) The mean will equal 1, and the median will be larger than 1.
(D) The mean and the median will be larger than 1.

246. Joe has kept track of how many new movies he has seen each year for the past 5 years. The greatest number of new movies he saw in these years was 20, while the median number of new movies he saw was 14. If the least number of new movies he saw in any of these years was 10, which of the following could be the average number of movies he has seen per year over the past 5 years?

(A) 10
(B) 12
(C) 13
(D) 14

247. The probability of selecting a random integer between the consecutive positive integers x and y inclusive is $\frac{1}{122}$. What is the smallest possible value of y?

248. The school basketball games cost $15 to attend. A season pass costs $170. What is the highest number of games that could be attended before spending more than the cost of the season pass?

(A) 10
(B) 11
(C) 12
(D) 17

249. In a list of eight numbers, each value is 10 more than the previous value. If the smallest value in the list is 15, what is the median of the list?

(A) 40
(B) 45
(C) 50
(D) 55

250. The scale of a map indicates that 1 cm is equal to 18 km in the real world. If two towns are 234 km apart, then what is their distance on the map in cm?

(A) 13
(B) 15
(C) 16
(D) 130

251. The probability of randomly selecting a green marble from a jar containing green, red, and blue marbles is $\dfrac{2}{9}$. What is the probability of randomly selecting a red or blue marble from the jar?

(A) $\dfrac{1}{3}$

(B) $\dfrac{4}{9}$

(C) $\dfrac{2}{3}$

(D) $\dfrac{7}{9}$

252. A school club has 3 freshmen, 2 sophomores, and 10 juniors as members. If a member is randomly selected to represent the club at an after-school function, what is the probability the selected member is a sophomore?

(A) $\dfrac{1}{15}$

(B) $\dfrac{2}{15}$

(C) $\dfrac{2}{15}$

(D) $\dfrac{1}{4}$

253. What is the average of $\sqrt{2}$ and $5\sqrt{2}$?

(A) $\sqrt{2}$

(B) $3\sqrt{2}$

(C) 3

(D) $\dfrac{9}{2}$

254. The median of a list of 12 numbers is $\dfrac{7}{4}$. When the list of numbers is written in order from smallest to largest, the sixth and seventh numbers have the same value. What is the value of the sixth number?

255. The regular rate for guitar lessons is $45 per lesson. The instructor currently offers a special package of $200 for six lessons. What percentage does a student save for six sessions by using this offer? Round your answer to the nearest whole percent.

(A) 20%

(B) 22%

(C) 24%

(D) 26%

256. The median of a set of six consecutive integers is $\dfrac{29}{2}$. What is the value of the smallest integer in the set?

257. In a bag containing only two colors of marbles, the ratio of red marbles to green marbles is 2:3. If there are 800 marbles in the bag, how many are red?

(A) 270
(B) 320
(C) 480
(D) 530

258. In a club with x members, 75% regularly attend meetings and 20% of the members are considered senior members. In terms of x, which of the following best represents the number of senior members who regularly attend meetings?

(A) $0.15x$
(B) $0.25x$
(C) $0.35x$
(D) $0.75x$

259. If x is a positive number, which of the following is equivalent to x% of 125?

(A) $\dfrac{5x}{4}$

(B) $\dfrac{25x}{4}$

(C) $\dfrac{5}{4x}$

(D) $\dfrac{5}{8x}$

260. Players A, B, C, and D are the favorites to win the U.S. Open. The odds of them winning based on the projections, in order, are 1:8, 1:4, 1:3, and 1:6. What is the probability of one of these players winning the U.S. Open?

(A) $\dfrac{5}{6}$

(B) $\dfrac{7}{8}$

(C) $\dfrac{8}{9}$

(D) $\dfrac{23}{24}$

261. If x and y are real numbers, which of the following is equivalent to 45% of $6x + 10y$?

(A) $\dfrac{x+y}{100}$

(B) $\dfrac{9x+9y}{2}$

(C) $\dfrac{27x+45x}{10}$

(D) $\dfrac{54x+90y}{2}$

262. The price of a single piece of furniture was increased by 25%. After the increase, five pieces of the furniture were sold for a total of $675. To the nearest cent, what was the original price of a single piece of this type of furniture?

(A) $101.25
(B) $108.00
(C) $126.56
(D) $135.00

263. If $\dfrac{a}{b} = \dfrac{3}{11}$, then what does $\dfrac{a+b}{b}$ equal?

(A) $\dfrac{8}{11}$

(B) $\dfrac{14}{11}$

(C) 4

(D) 11

264. In a set containing n numbers, 40% are divisible by a positive integer k. Which of the following represents the fraction of numbers in the set that have a nonzero remainder when divided by k?

(A) $\dfrac{1}{5}$

(B) $\dfrac{2}{5}$

(C) $\dfrac{3}{5}$

(D) $\dfrac{4}{5}$

265. When a number x is increased by 40%, the resulting value is 92. If x is decreased by 10%, then the resulting value is

(A) $\dfrac{23}{10}$

(B) $\dfrac{230}{7}$

(C) $\dfrac{184}{5}$

(D) $\dfrac{414}{7}$

266. A special set of 200 cards contains blue and green cards only. If the set contains 54 more blue cards than green cards, then what percentage of the deck is made up of green cards?
(A) 27%
(B) 36.5%
(C) 41.2%
(D) 63.5%

267. In a meeting of junior and senior high school students, the ratio of juniors to seniors is 1:3. Each of the following could be the total number of students at the meeting *except*
(A) 16
(B) 52
(C) 58
(D) 60

268. Exactly 2 years ago, a student purchased 10 shares of a stock. In the first year, the value increased by 3%. In the second year, the price increased by another 5%. If the student originally paid $140.60 for the 10 shares, then what is the current price of a single share to the nearest dollar?

269. If $\dfrac{1}{4}$% of x is 19, then what does x equal?
(A) 7.6
(B) 76
(C) 760
(D) 7600

270. Suppose for two variables x and y that when $x = \sqrt{2}$, $y = 4$. If y is directly proportional to x, then which of the following equations describes their relationship?

(A) $y = \dfrac{\sqrt{2}}{4}x$

(B) $y = \dfrac{\sqrt{2}}{2}x$

(C) $y = 2\sqrt{2}x$

(D) $y = 4\sqrt{2}x$

271. Which of the following is the visual representation of the line $y = 2x - 3$?

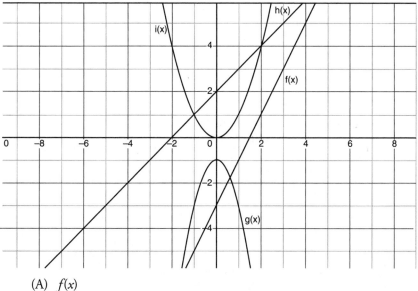

(A) $f(x)$
(B) $g(x)$
(C) $h(x)$
(D) $i(x)$

272. During a sale, customers can purchase 1 pound of apples at a 15% discount. Customers may also use a coupon to receive an additional 2% off the sale price. If the price of a pound of apples before the sale was x, which of the following represents the price paid during the sale if the coupon is used?

(A) $\dfrac{3x}{1000}$

(B) $\dfrac{13x}{1000}$

(C) $\dfrac{147x}{1000}$

(D) $\dfrac{833x}{1000}$

273. If x is greater than $\dfrac{1}{8}$ % of 2115, then which of the following is the smallest possible integer value of x?

(A) 2
(B) 3
(C) 8
(D) 26

274. If Bobby can run 3 miles in 20 minutes and Aiden can run 3 miles in 25 minutes, what is the difference in the number of miles they can run in 100 minutes?

(A) 0
(B) 3
(C) 12
(D) 15

275. A customer purchases items from a grocery store totaling $34.90. If he uses a loyalty card that provides a discount and must only pay $31.41, then what percentage discount did he receive?

276. Sales tax is 6%. If the sales tax came to $0.87, what was the total cost of the meal before tax?

(A) $11.30
(B) $5.22
(C) $14.50
(D) $16.90

277. Tutor A charges a student $90 for 3 hours of tutoring, while tutor B charges a student $40 for 1 hour of tutoring. Which of the following is the ratio of the hourly rate for tutor A to the hourly rate of tutor B?

(A) 1:2
(B) 2:3
(C) 1:4
(D) 3:4

278. If m varies directly as n, and $m = 6a$ when $n = a$, then what is the value of m when $n = 3$?

279. If b varies directly as $a^2 + 1$, and $b = 10$ when $a = 2$, then when $a = 5$, what is b?

280. In a right triangle A, the hypotenuse has a length of 8 and the smallest interior angle is 30 degrees. In another right triangle B, the smallest interior angle is also 30 degrees but the hypotenuse has a length of 2. What is the ratio of the area of triangle A to the area of triangle B?

(A) 2:1
(B) 4:1
(C) 16:1
(D) 32:1

281. John won an open Congressional seat in a two-person race by 1,254 votes. If John won the race by 56%, and all the votes were cast and counted for either John or his opponent, then what was the total number of votes cast?

(A) 8,350
(B) 9,150
(C) 10,450
(D) 12,510

282. If the value of x decreases by 12%, its value is a. If the original value of x increases by 10%, its value is b. In terms of x, what is the value of $a - b$?

(A) $-0.22x$
(B) $-0.02x$
(C) $0.98x$
(D) $x - 0.02$

283. The average of $3x$, $5x$, $2x - 1$, and $x + 1$ is 8. What is the average of x and $x + 2$?

(A) $\dfrac{12}{11}$

(B) $\dfrac{32}{11}$

(C) $\dfrac{43}{11}$

(D) $\dfrac{48}{11}$

284. If the length of a single side of a cube is x, what is the ratio of the area of a single face of the cube to the volume of the cube?

(A) $1:x$

(B) $1:x^2$

(C) $1:x^3$

(D) $1:x^4$

285. If the ratio of m to n is 2:9, then the ratio of $18m$ to n is

(A) 4:1

(B) 9:1

(C) 12:1

(D) 16:1

286. In a bag of marbles, there are 15% more red marbles than blue marbles. If the bag contains only these two colors of marbles, then which of the following is a possible value for the total number of marbles in the bag?

(A) 165

(B) 245

(C) 310

(D) 430

287. If t is inversely proportional to r, and $t = 6$ when $r = 2$, then when $r = \dfrac{1}{4}$, what is t?

288. If the difference between 25% of x and 20% of x is 14, then what is the value of x?

289. The ratio of Frank's hourly pay to Rich's hourly pay is 5:6. If after 2 hours of work, Frank and Rich are paid a total of $66, what is Rich's hourly pay?

(A) $12
(B) $15
(C) $18
(D) $22

290. Suppose y varies inversely as x and when $x = 12n$, $y = \dfrac{1}{2}n$ for some nonzero n. In terms of n, what is the value of y when $x = 2n$?

(A) $\dfrac{n}{4}$

(B) $\dfrac{n}{2}$

(C) $2n$

(D) $4n$

291. If x and y are positive numbers such that $x\%$ of y is a, then in terms of a, what is $y\%$ of x?

(A) $\dfrac{a}{100}$

(B) $\dfrac{a}{50}$

(C) $\dfrac{a}{10}$

(D) a

292. A scale model of a square-shaped garden is to be built such that each foot of length in the scale model represents 100 feet in the actual garden. If the garden has an area of 62,500 square feet, what will be the area of the scale model, in square feet?

(A) 5.5
(B) 6.25
(C) 550
(D) 625

293. At a construction site, x nails are used every 6 hours. In terms of x, how many nails are used in 20 hours?

(A) $\dfrac{10x}{3}$

(B) $\dfrac{20x}{3}$

(C) $\dfrac{26x}{3}$

(D) $20x$

294. At a retail establishment, the number of employees required on shift is directly proportional to the number of people entering the building during the shift. If the establishment required 20 employees during a shift when 850 people entered the building, how many employees will be required when it is estimated that 340 customers enter the building during their shift?

(A) 4
(B) 8
(C) 14
(D) 28

295. For every five $10 bills, a wallet contains fifteen $1 bills. Which of the following is the ratio of $10 bills to $1 bills in the wallet?

(A) 1:2
(B) 1:3
(C) 10:1
(D) 10:3

296. In a group of first graders, x say that green is their favorite color. When asked an hour later, three of them change their minds and decide that green is no longer their favorite color. If there are y first graders in the group, which of the following represents the percentage that now say green is their favorite color?

(A) $100\left(\dfrac{x}{y} - 3\right)\%$

(B) $100\left(\dfrac{x}{y} + 3\right)\%$

(C) $\dfrac{100(x-3)}{y}\%$

(D) $\dfrac{100x}{y+3}\%$

297. What is the probability of selecting the letter N from a bag containing the letters PENNSYLVANIA?

298. If x and y are positive numbers, which of the following represents $(x + y)\%$ of $\dfrac{50}{x^2 + 2xy + y^2}$?

(A) $\dfrac{1}{2}(x - y)$

(B) $2(x + y)$

(C) $\dfrac{1}{2(x + y)}$

(D) $\dfrac{2(x + y)}{x - y}$

299. If 64% of students in a class earn a grade of B or higher, what fraction of students earn a grade of C or lower?

(A) $\dfrac{4}{25}$

(B) $\dfrac{9}{25}$

(C) $\dfrac{12}{25}$

(D) $\dfrac{16}{25}$

300. If the ratio of a to b is 3:17, then what is the value of b when $a = \dfrac{9}{2}$?

301. The value of an antique decreases by 8% one year and by 2% the next. After this, to the nearest tenth of a percent, the antique is worth what percentage of its original value?

(A) 10.0%
(B) 16.0%
(C) 18.4%
(D) 90.2%

302. A club saw an 8% increase in the number of members over a 1-month period. If before the increase there were 250 members in the club, how many members are in the club at month's end?

(A) 262
(B) 270
(C) 275
(D) 286

303. The price of item *A* is $\$m$, and the price of item *B* is $\$n$. If item *A* goes on sale for 10% off and item *B* goes on sale for 20% off, which of the following represents the cost of buying both items while they are on sale, in dollars?

(A) $\dfrac{m+n}{5}$

(B) $\dfrac{3m+2n}{10}$

(C) $\dfrac{9m+8n}{10}$

(D) $10m + 20n$

304. If *x* is 5% of $\dfrac{1}{4}$, then *x* =

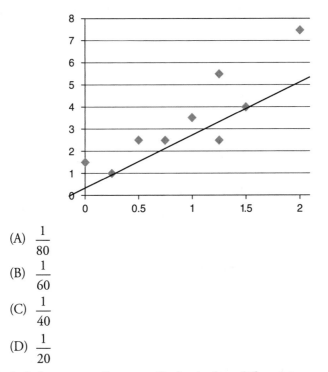

(A) $\dfrac{1}{80}$

(B) $\dfrac{1}{60}$

(C) $\dfrac{1}{40}$

(D) $\dfrac{1}{20}$

305. A clothing store sells a type of jacket in three different sizes: small, medium, and large. Of the store's entire stock of this jacket, 10% are small and 40% are medium. If there are 170 jackets in stock, how many are large?

306. If $\dfrac{1}{8} y = x$, and both are nonzero, then what percent of y is x?

(A) 8%
(B) 12.5%
(C) 125%
(D) 800%

307. A sea turtle buries 90 eggs in the sand. Of these, 50 eggs hatch, and of those, 37 do not make it to the ocean. What is the probability an egg chosen at random hatched and the baby turtle made it to the ocean?

(A) $\dfrac{37}{90}$

(B) $\dfrac{13}{50}$

(C) $\dfrac{13}{90}$

(D) $\dfrac{13}{37}$

308. The ratio of the numbers x, y, and z is 1:3:5. If $y = x + 1$, what is the value of z?

309. A particle's path and speed can be represented in the xy-coordinate plane by movement along the x-axis at a rate of 4 units every 20 minutes. If the start of the particle's path is represented by the origin and it moves in the positive direction, at which of the following points is the particle located after 50 minutes?

(A) (3, 0)
(B) (8, 0)
(C) (10, 0)
(D) (20, 0)

310. Which of the following values most accurately reflects the average rate of change between the variables based on the line of best fit in the graph?

(A) $\dfrac{3}{8}$

(B) $\dfrac{3}{4}$

(C) $\dfrac{4}{3}$

(D) $\dfrac{12}{5}$

Passport to Advanced Math

Passport to Advanced Math focuses on the next level of algebraic math, nonlinear expressions and functions in which a variable has an exponent that is not 0 or 1. You will be working with straightforward expressions, word problems, equations, exponents, polynomials, functions, and graphs. Advanced Math questions do not appear in the no-calculator sections; however, that does not mean a calculator is needed to solve every problem. In some cases, it is more efficient to solve the problems without a calculator.

Topics

- Quadratic equations
- Nonlinear expressions
- Polynomial factors and graphs
- Linear and quadratic systems
- Functions
- Radicals and rational exponents
- Nonlinear equation graphs

Skills

- Solve equations by factoring.
- Rewrite equations in another form.
- Add, subtract, multiply, and divide rational and polynomial expressions and simplify.
- Match graphs to equations.
- Determine the equation of a curve from a graph.
- Determine how a graph would change if its equation changed.

Need to Know

- Quadratic Equations
  - Solve for x when given the polynomial $ax^2 + bx + c$.
  - Use the quadratic formula $x = \dfrac{-b \pm \sqrt{b^2 - 4ac}}{2a}$ and substitute for x.
  - Don't forget! You need to complete two equations for each polynomial:

    $$x = \frac{-b + \sqrt{b^2 - 4ac}}{2a} \quad \text{and} \quad x = \frac{-b - \sqrt{b^2 - 4ac}}{2a}$$

- Factoring Polynomials: To factor polynomials, you are essentially deconstructing an equation:
  - Using the Greatest Common Factor (GCF)
    - In the expression $2x - 14$, the GCF is 2. Factor out the GCF: $\dfrac{2x - 14}{2} = 2(x - 7)$
    - In the expression $15x^3 + 9x^2$, the GCF is $3x^2$. Factor out the GCF:

      $$\frac{15x^3 + 9x^2}{3x^2} = 3x^2(5x + 3)$$

  - Using difference of squares, difference of cubes, or sum of cubes for binomials
    - $a^2 - b^2 = (a + b)(a - b)$
    - $a^4 - 25 = (a^2 + 5)(a^2 - 5)$
  - Using FOIL for trinomials (First Inside Outside Last). This is essentially the reverse of the distributive property.
- Graphs of Quadratic Functions
  - Standard form: $y = ax^2 + bx + c$
  - Intercept form: $y = a(x - m)(x - n)$, where m and n are the x-intercepts and $f(x) = 0$.
  - Vertex form: $y = a(x - h)^2 + k$, where (h, k) are the coordinates of the vertex of the parabola.

Complete Questions 311–444 with the use of a calculator when needed.

311. If $xy^2 = 4$, what is the value of $\dfrac{2x^3 y^4 - x^2 y^2}{x^2 y^2}$?

    (A) 3
    (B) 4
    (C) 7
    (D) 8

312. Which of the following is equivalent to $9m - 6m + 1$?

(A) $3m + 1$
(B) $3m - 1$
(C) $(3m + 1)^2$
(D) $(3m - 1)^2$

313. If $2x^2 - y + 1 = 15$, what is the value of $2x^2 - y - 7$?

(A) -7
(B) -6
(C) 7
(D) 8

314. Which of the following is equivalent to $\left(\dfrac{1}{5}x - y\right)^2$?

(A) $\dfrac{1}{25}\left(x^2 - y^2\right)$

(B) $\dfrac{1}{25}x^2 + y^2$

(C) $\dfrac{1}{25}x^2 - \dfrac{2}{5}xy + y^2$

(D) $\dfrac{1}{25}x^2 + \dfrac{2}{5}xy + y^2$

315. Which of the following must be larger than $a^2 - 2ab$ for all real values of a and b?

I. $(a - b)^2$
II. $a(a - 2b)$
III. $a - 2b$

(A) I only
(B) II only
(C) III only
(D) I, II, and III

316. Which of the following is equivalent to $ab^3 - ab^4 + a^2b^2$?

(A) $ab(b^2 - b^3 + ab)$
(B) $ab(ab^2 - ab^3 + ab)$
(C) $ab(b^2 - b^3 + 1)$
(D) $ab(b^3 - b^4 + 1)$

317. Which of the following functions has three distinct 0s?

(A) $f(x) = x^2$
(B) $f(x) = x^3$
(C) $f(x) = x(x - 4)^2$
(D) $f(x) = x(x + 4)(x - 4)$

318. What is the maximum y value reached by the graph of $f(x) = -x^2 - 5$?

(A) -5
(B) -4
(C) -2
(D) 1

319. If $a^3(a^2 - 1) = 0$, then which of the following is a possible value of a?

(A) -8
(B) -2
(C) 0
(D) 2

320. If $f(x) = x^2 - x$, then which of the following represents $f(c + 1)$?

(A) $c^2 - 1$
(B) $c^2 + 1$
(C) $c^2 + c$
(D) $c^2 + c - 1$

321. What is the largest value of x that makes the equation $3x^2 - 16x = -5$ true?

322. If $g(x) = \dfrac{x - 6}{x^2}$ for all nonzero x, then $g(-1) =$

(A) -7
(B) -5
(C) 5
(D) 7

323. If $f(x) = x + 5$, then $f\left(\dfrac{1}{8}k + 6\right) =$

(A) $\dfrac{15}{4}k$

(B) $\dfrac{15}{4}k + 11$

(C) $\dfrac{5}{8}k + 30$

(D) $\dfrac{1}{8}k + 11$

324. If the graph of $f(x)$ is as pictured, which of the following could be the graph of $f(x - 2)$?

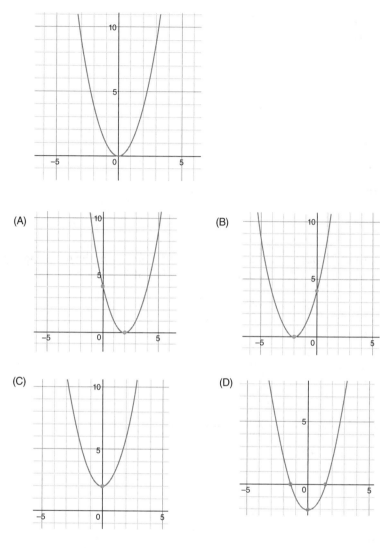

325. Given the graph of a function f in the following figure, what is the value of $f(1) + f(3)$?

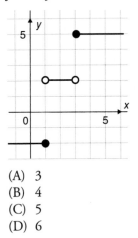

(A) 3
(B) 4
(C) 5
(D) 6

326. Given the graph of a function $f(x) = ax^2 + bx + c$ in the following figure, which of the following statements must be true?

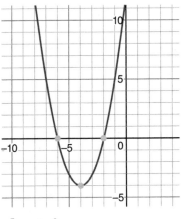

   I. $a > 0$
  II. $b \neq 0$
 III. $c = 0$

(A) I only
(B) II only
(C) III only
(D) I and II only

327. Given the graph of the function $g(x)$ in the following figure, for which values of x is $g(x) > 0$?

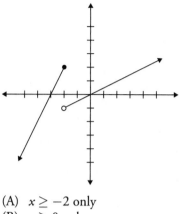

(A) $x \geq -2$ only
(B) $x \geq 0$ only
(C) $-3 < x \leq -2$ only
(D) $-3 < x \leq -2$ and $x > 0$

328. If the graph of a quadratic function $f(x) = ax^2 + bx + c$ has intercepts at $(4, 0)$, $(-3, 0)$, and $(12, 0)$, then $b =$
(A) -12
(B) -1
(C) 0
(D) 1

329. Given the function $f(x) = x - 8$, if $n > 2$, then $f(n)$ must be greater than
(A) -14
(B) -12
(C) -8
(D) -6

330. If $g(x) = \dfrac{x+1}{x}$ for all nonzero x and $g(k+1) = 3$, then which of the following is the value of k?

(A) $-\dfrac{4}{3}$

(B) $-\dfrac{1}{2}$

(C) $-\dfrac{1}{3}$

(D) $-\dfrac{1}{4}$

331. A function $k(x)$ is defined such that if x is even, $k(x)$ is 4, and if x is odd, $k(x)$ is 6. What is the value of $k(1) + k(2)$?

(A) 2
(B) 4
(C) 6
(D) 10

332. The graph of a quadratic function does not cross the x-axis and has a maximum at the point $(0, -4)$. Which of the following is a possible equation for the described function?

(A) $f(x) = -\dfrac{3}{4}x^2 - 4$

(B) $f(x) = -\dfrac{1}{2}x^2 + 4$

(C) $f(x) = 4x^2 - 4$

(D) $f(x) = x^2 + 4$

333. The graph of a quadratic function can be seen here. Which of the following is the function that describes it?

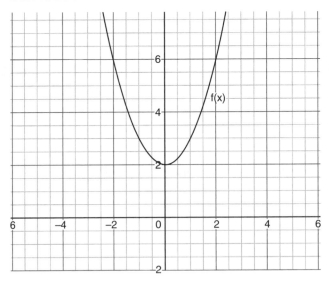

(A) $f(x) = -x^2 + 2$
(B) $f(x) = -x^2 + x + 1$
(C) $f(x) = x^2 + 2$
(D) $f(x) = 2x^2 + x + 2$

334. If $f(x) = \dfrac{1}{3}x + 5$ and $g(x) = f(x) - 1$, then the slope of the graph of

$g(x)$ must be

(A) -5

(B) -3

(C) $\dfrac{1}{5}$

(D) $\dfrac{1}{3}$

335. If points A and C of triangle ABC in the following figure lie on the graph of $h(x) = x^2 - 8$, then which of the following is the area of triangle ABC?

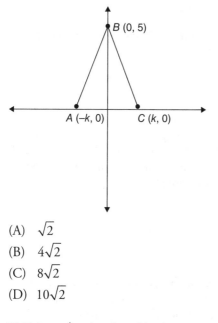

(A) $\sqrt{2}$

(B) $4\sqrt{2}$

(C) $8\sqrt{2}$

(D) $10\sqrt{2}$

336. If $f(n) = n^4 - 4n$, then $f(-1) =$

(A) -8

(B) 4

(C) 5

(D) 8

337. If the point $(-1, 5)$ is on the graph of a function $g(x)$, and $h(x) - g(x) - k$ for some constant k, then which of the following points must be on the graph of $h(x)$?

(A) $(-k, 5h)$

(B) $(-1, 5 - k)$

(C) $(k - 1, 5)$

(D) $(-1 - k, 5)$

338. The graphs of $f(x) = x^2 + 1$ and $g(x) = kx^2$ intersect at the point $\left(\dfrac{\sqrt{2}}{2}, n \right)$ for some constant n. What is the value of k?

(A) 1

(B) 2

(C) 3

(D) 4

339. If $f(x) = 3x^2 - 4$ and $g(x) = \dfrac{1}{2} f(x) + 4$, then what is the value of $g(4)$?

(A) 18

(B) 20

(C) 26

(D) 28

340. The number of lines of code $c(h)$ a programmer wrote per hour h over a 12-hour period can be described by the function $c(h) = -h^2 + 12h$ for $0 \le h \le 12$. What was the maximum number of lines of code the programmer wrote during any one hour?

(A) 6

(B) 8

(C) 24

(D) 36

341. If the value of a car y years after purchase can be represented by the function $V(y) = 5000(0.92)^y$, to the nearest cent, which of the following is the value of the car 8 years after its purchase?

(A) $2023.68

(B) $2566.09

(C) $3317.10

(D) $3680.00

342. If the point $(3, 9)$ lies on the graph of $f(x) = x^3 + x^2 - n$, what is the value of n?

343. Given the function $h(x) = \dfrac{x-1}{4}$, if $h(x+3) = 5$, what is the value of x?

(A) 14

(B) 16

(C) 18

(D) 21

344. If the graph of $f(x)$ crosses the x-axis at a single point $(4, 0)$, then at what point will the graph of $f(x-6)$ cross the x-axis?

(A) $(-10, 0)$

(B) $(-6, 0)$

(C) $(-2, 0)$

(D) $(10, 0)$

345. If the graph of $f(x) = (x-4)(x+1)(x+6)(x-9)$ crosses the x-axis at the point $(a, 0)$, then each of the following is a possible value of a *except*

(A) -6

(B) -4

(C) -1

(D) 9

346. If $g(x) = x(x-1)^2$, then at how many unique values of x does $g(x) = 0$?

(A) None

(B) 1

(C) 2

(D) 3

347. What is the value of the largest zero of the function $f(x) = x^2 - 4x - 5$?

348. If $f(x) = x^2 + 2x + n$, $g(x) = x^2 - x$, and the intercept point is $(-1, 2)$, then what is the value of n?

(A) -1

(B) 1

(C) 2

(D) 3

349. The points $(-2, 0)$ and $(6, 0)$ lie on the graph of a quadratic function $f(x)$. Which of the following could be equivalent to $f(x)$?

(A) $x^2 + 4x - 12$

(B) $x^2 - 2x + 6$

(C) $x^2 + 8x + 12$

(D) $x^2 - 4x - 12$

350. If $f(x) = \dfrac{4}{5}x^2$ and $g(x) = \dfrac{1}{2}x + \dfrac{1}{2}$, then which of the following is equivalent to $g(f(x))$?

(A) $\dfrac{2}{5}x^2 + \dfrac{1}{2}$

(B) $\dfrac{4}{7}x^2 + \dfrac{1}{2}$

(C) $\dfrac{4}{9}x^2 + \dfrac{4}{9}$

(D) $\dfrac{1}{5}x^2 + \dfrac{1}{5}x + \dfrac{1}{5}$

351. Given the following graph of the function $f(x)$, which of the following statements must be true for all values of x?

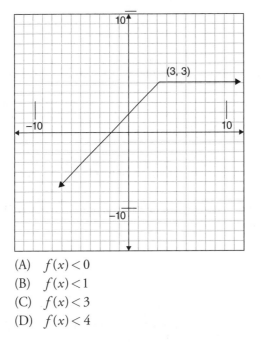

(A) $f(x) < 0$
(B) $f(x) < 1$
(C) $f(x) < 3$
(D) $f(x) < 4$

352. If the graph of $g(x)$ is a vertical translation of the graph of $f(x) = -x^2 + 1$, then which of the following has the largest value?

(A) $g(-3)$

(B) $g(-2)$

(C) $g(-1)$

(D) $g(0)$

353. Which of the following represents all the solutions to the equation $k(x) = 0$ when $k(x) = x^3(x^2 - 4x + 4)$?

(A) $x = 0$

(B) $x = 2$

(C) $x = 0$ and $x = 2$

(D) $x = 0$ and $x = -2$

354. If a and b are two distinct numbers that make the equation $n^2 - 8n = 9$ true, then what is the value of $a + b$?

(A) -8

(B) -6

(C) 6

(D) 8

355. Given the following graph of the function $f(x)$, for what values of x is $f(x) > 0$?

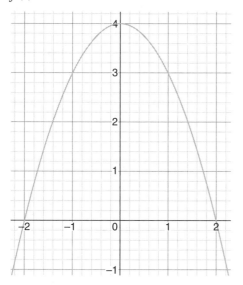

(A) $x < -2$ only
(B) $x > 2$ only
(C) $-2 < x < 2$ only
(D) $0 < x < 4$ only

356. Which of the following statements best describes the graph of a quadratic function $f(x) = ax^2 + bx + c$ where $a > 0$?

(A) The graph has a single minimum value and crosses the x-axis at two distinct points.
(B) The graph has a single minimum value and may or may not cross the x-axis.
(C) The graph has a single maximum value and crosses the x-axis at two distinct points.
(D) The graph has a single maximum value and may or may not cross the x-axis.

357. What is the largest possible number n such that the graphs of $h(x) = x^2 + 3x - 8$ and $k(x) = -4$ intersect at the point (n, y)?

(A) 1
(B) 2
(C) 4
(D) 6

358. If $f(x) = 3x$ and $5f(x) = f(x)$, then $x =$

(A) $\dfrac{1}{5}$

(B) $\dfrac{1}{3}$

(C) 0
(D) 4

359. If for all x, $g(m) = 2m - m^3$, what is the value of $g(-2)$?

(A) -12
(B) -10
(C) -8
(D) 4

360. The graph of a quadratic function $f(x) = ax^2 + bx + c$ reaches a minimum value at a point (x, y). Which of the following inequalities must be true?

(A) $a > 0$

(B) $a < 0$

(C) $a > b$

(D) $a < b$

361. Which of the following will shift the graph of $f(x)$ two units downward on the y-axis?

(A) $f(x + 2)$

(B) $f(x - 2)$

(C) $f(x) + 2$

(D) $f(x) - 2$

362. If $f(x) = \dfrac{x^2 - x}{2}$, then which of the following is equivalent to $f(2a - 1)$?

(A) $2a^2 - 1$

(B) $2a^2 - 3a$

(C) $2a^2 - 6a$

(D) $2a^2 - 3a + 1$

363. If $c > 0$ and $f(x) = 2x - 9$, then which of the following inequalities must be true?

(A) $f(c) > -9$

(B) $f(c) > -2$

(C) $f(c) > 0$

(D) $f(c) > \dfrac{9}{2}$

364. Which of the following functions will have the smallest minimum value?

(A) $f(x) = x^2 - 2x + 3$
(B) $g(x) = x^2 + 3x - 1$
(C) $h(x) = 2x^2 + x + 3$
(D) $i(x) = x^2 - 2x - 3$

365. The height, in meters, of a particle when t seconds have passed can be expressed as the function $f(t) = -2t^2 + 32$ for $0 \le t \le 4$. In meters, what is the height of the particle when 2 seconds have passed?

366. For a function $g(x) = x^3 - kx + c$, $g(-1) = 4$ and $g(0) = 10$. What is the value of $k + c$?

(A) -9
(B) -5
(C) 5
(D) 9

367. The following table represents values of a quadratic function $f(x) = ax^2 + bx + c$ for selected values of x. What is the value of the product bc?

x	-3	-2	-1	0
$f(x)$	2	0	0	2

368. If $f(x) = -x^2 + 10x - 21$, then at how many points in the xy-plane do the graphs of $f(x)$ and $g(x) = -f(x)$ intersect?

(A) 0
(B) 1
(C) 2
(D) 3

369. If $f(x) = 5x\sqrt{k}$ and $f(\sqrt{k}) = 35$, then what is the value of k?

370. The point $(3, y)$ lies on the graph of the function $h(x) = 4x^2 - x^3$. What is the value of y?

(A) 3
(B) 6
(C) 9
(D) 12

371. For a function $f(x) = x^2 - 3$ and a constant m, $f(2m+1) = 3m$. Which of the following is the value of $4m^2 + m$?

(A) -4
(B) -3
(C) 0
(D) 2

372. For a number k, $g\left(\dfrac{k}{2}\right) = 3k - 2$. Which of the following is equivalent to $g(4k)$?

(A) $6k - 4$
(B) $8k - 2$
(C) $16k - 4$
(D) $24k - 2$

373. The following figure shows the graph of the function $f(x)$. What is the value of $f(2) + f(4)$?

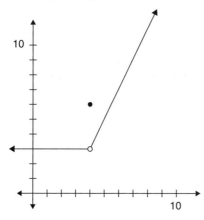

374. The points $(0, 5)$ and $(8, 8)$ lie on the graph of a function $k(x)$. If the points $(-5, 5)$ and $(3, 8)$ lie on the graph of $k(x+m)+n$, then what is the value of $m + n$?

(A) -5
(B) -3
(C) 3
(D) 5

375. Given the functions $f(a) = a - 1$ and $g(a) = a - 2$, for what value(s) of a does $\dfrac{1}{6} f(a) = \dfrac{1}{g(a)}$?

(A) -1 only

(B) $\dfrac{1}{4}$ only

(C) $\dfrac{7}{6}$ only

(D) 4 and -1 only

376. The value of a function f for a given number is found by squaring the difference of that number and 3 and then adding 4. Which of the following is equivalent to $f(x)$?

(A) $x^2 - 5$
(B) $x^2 - 6x + 13$
(C) $x^2 + 13$
(D) $x^2 - 3x + 13$

377. If the point $\left(x, \dfrac{3}{2}\right)$ lies on the graph of $k(x) = \dfrac{1}{2}(x-1)^2$ and $x > 0$, then $x =$

(A) $\dfrac{1}{8}$

(B) $\dfrac{13}{8}$

(C) $1 + \sqrt{3}$

(D) $\dfrac{\sqrt{6}}{4}$

378. If the point $(-2, 8)$ is on the graph of $f(x) = cx^3$, then $c =$
(A) -1
(B) 0
(C) 1
(D) 2

379. If the graph of a function $f(x)$ never intersects the line $y = 2$, which of the following statements must be true?

   I. There is no value x such that $f(x) = 0$.
   II. There is no value x such that $f(x) = 2$.
   III. The function is undefined at the point $x = 2$.

(A) I only
(B) II only
(C) III only
(D) I and II only

380. A function $g(x)$ is defined such that for a function $f(x)$, $g(x) = \dfrac{f(x)}{8}$. If for a constant a, $g(a) = 3$, what is the value of $f(a)$?

381. If $g(x) = \dfrac{|x-1|}{x-1}$ and $x > 1$, which of the following is equivalent to $g(x)$?

(A) -1
(B) 1

(C) $-\dfrac{1}{x-1}$

(D) $\dfrac{1}{x-1}$

382. A function $f(x)$ is defined for all real values of x. If $f(12) = 11$, then what is the value of $f(13)$?

(A) 11
(B) 12
(C) 13
(D) This cannot be determined from the information given.

383. The graph of $g(x)$ is found by translating the graph of $f(x)$ to the left 1 unit and up 4 units. Which of the following defines $g(x)$ in terms of $f(x)$?

(A) $f(x+1) + 4$
(B) $f(x-1) + 4$
(C) $f(x-1) + 1$
(D) $f(x+4) - 1$

384. What is the value of $\dfrac{(f(2))^2}{2}$ if $f(b) = b + b^2$?

385. The graphs of $f(x) = -x^2 + 9$ and $g(x) = x^2 - 9$ intersect at the point (x, y), where x and y are nonnegative. What is the value of $x + y$?

(A) -6
(B) -3
(C) 3
(D) 6

386. The following graph is of the function $g(x) = \dfrac{1}{2} f(x) + 6$ for $x > 0$, where $f(x) = x^2$. What is the value of b?

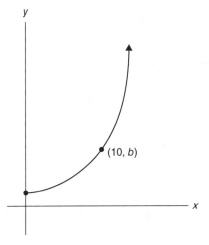

387. For the two functions, $f(x)$ and $g(x)$, tables of values are shown below. What is the value of $g(f(3))$?

x	$f(x)$
-5	7
-2	-5
1	3
3	2

x	$g(x)$
-2	3
1	-1
2	-3
3	-5

(A) -5
(B) -3
(C) -1
(D) 2

388. Listed below are five functions, each denoted $g(x)$ and each involving a real-number constant $c > 1$. If $f(x) = 2x$, which of these four functions yields the greatest value for $f(g(x))$, for all $x > 1$?

(A) $g(x) = \dfrac{c}{x}$

(B) $g(x) = x - c$

(C) $g(x) = \dfrac{x}{c}$

(D) $g(x) = cx$

389. The imaginary number i is defined such that $i^2 = -1$. What does

$i + i^2 + i^3 + \cdots + i^{23}$ equal?

(A) i
(B) $-i$
(C) -1
(D) 0

390. The imaginary number i is defined such that $i^2 = -1$. What does $i^5 - i^2$ equal?

(A) $i + 1$
(B) $1 - i$
(C) 1
(D) -1

391. Which statement is true about the given numbers?

Column A	Column B
The positive value of x in	The positive value of x in
$2x^2 - 14 = 18$	$2x^2 + 14 = 46$

(A) The number in column A is greater.
(B) The number is column B is greater.
(C) The two numbers are equal.
(D) The relationship cannot be determined by the information given.

392. Which value represents the linear term in $y = (x+1)(x-6) - 6x^2$?

(A) $-35x$
(B) $-5x$
(C) $6x$
(D) $35x$

393. Factor the quadratic expression $2x^2 + 5x + 3$.

(A) $x(2x + 5) = 3$

(B) $(2x + 3)(x + 1)$

(C) $(x + 3)(2x - 1)$

(D) $(2x + 1)(x + 3)$

394. Find a quadratic function to model the values in the table.

x	y
-1	2
0	-2
3	10

(A) $y = -2x^2 + 2x - 2$

(B) $y = 2x^2 - 2x + 2$

(C) $y = 2x^2 - 2x - 2$

(D) $y = -2x + 2x + 2$

395. Which quadratic equation matches the following values $(-2, 8)$, $(0, -4)$, $(4, 68)$?

(A) $y = 4x^2 + 2x - 4$

(B) $y = 4x^2 - 2x + 4$

(C) $y = 2x^2 + 4x - 4$

(D) $y = -4x^2 - 2x + 8$

396. Which one of the following is a solution for $\frac{2}{3}t^2 - 7 = 17$?

(A) -6

(B) -4

(C) $\sqrt{15}$

(D) $\sqrt{24}$

397. Which one of the following is *not* a quadratic equation?

(A) $x^2 - 4 = 0$

(B) $-9 + x^2 = 0$

(C) $-7x + 12 = 0$

(D) $x^2 + 10x + 21 = 0$

398. What is the value of x when $3x^2 - 78 = 114$?

(A) $\pm 2\sqrt{3}$

(B) $\pm 4\sqrt{3}$

(C) ± 6

(D) ± 8

399. What is the *x*-coordinate of the vertex for the graph of the equation $y = -\dfrac{1}{2}x^2 - x + 8$?

(A) −2

(B) −1

(C) $\dfrac{1}{2}$

(D) 1

400. What are the *x*-intercepts of the graph $y = -x^2 - 6x + 40$?

(A) 4 and 10

(B) −7 and 1

(C) −10 and 4

(D) −8 and 2

401. Which of the following is a solution for $-3x^2 + 22x + 93 = 0$?

(A) −3

(B) $-\dfrac{6}{31}$

(C) 3

(D) $\dfrac{31}{6}$

402. Which one of the following is a solution for $4x^2 - 17x + 13 = 0$?

(A) −1

(B) $\dfrac{4}{13}$

(C) $\dfrac{17}{8}$

(D) $\dfrac{13}{4}$

403. Which of the following expressions is equal to $(5x^3 + 3x^2 - x + 1) - (2x^3 + x - 5)$?

(A) $3x^3 + 3x^2 - 2x - 4$

(B) $3x^3 + 3x^2 - 4$

(C) $3x^3 + 3x^2 - 2x + 6$

(D) $3x^3 + 3x^2 + 2x - 6$

404. Which of the following is equal to $\left(-x^2 - 5x + 7\right) + \left(-7x^2 + 5x - 2\right)$?

    (A) $6x^2 + 5$

    (B) $-8x^2 - 10x + 5$

    (C) $-8x^2 + 5$

    (D) $-6x^2 - 5$

405. A conservation study took a count of the number of migrating geese at a particular lake and recounted the lake's population of geese on each of the next 6 weeks. Find a quadratic function that models the data as a function of x, the number of weeks.

Week	0	1	2	3	4	5	6
Population	585	582	629	726	873	1070	1317

    (A) $P(x) = 25x^2 - 28x + 585$

    (B) $P(x) = 30x^2 + 28x + 535$

    (C) $P(x) = 25x^2 - 28x - 585$

    (D) $P(x) = 30x^2 - 28x - 535$

406. Which graph best fits the equation $y = -2(x - 2)^2 - 4$?

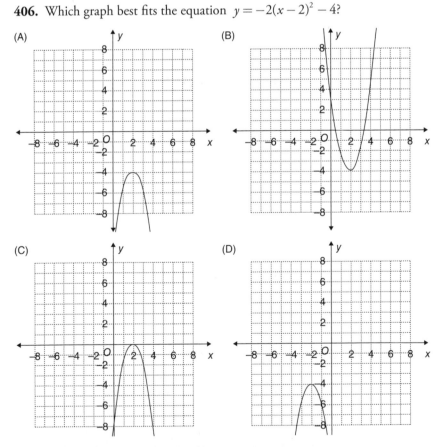

407. Identify the vertex and the *y*-intercept of the graph of the function
$y = -3(x+2)^2 + 5$.

(A) vertex: $(-2, 5)$; *y*-intercept: -7
(B) vertex: $(2, -5)$; *y*-intercept: -12
(C) vertex: $(2, 5)$; *y*-intercept: -7
(D) vertex: $(-2, -5)$; *y*-intercept: 9

408. The base of a triangular sail is *x* feet, and its height is $\frac{1}{2}x + 7$ feet. Which expression represents the sail's area?

(A) $\frac{1}{2}x^2 + 7x$

(B) $\frac{1}{2}x^2 + \frac{7}{2}x$

(C) $\frac{1}{4}x^2 + \frac{7}{2}x$

(D) $\frac{1}{4}x^2 + 7x$

409. Which of the following is equal to $(4x - 9)(7x - 2)$?

(A) $28x^2 - 71x - 18$
(B) $28x^2 - 55x + 18$
(C) $28x^2 + 55x + 18$
(D) $28x^2 - 71x + 15$

410. Which trinomial represents the area of the trapezoid?

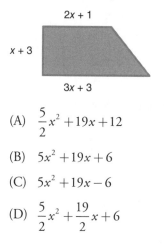

2x + 1

x + 3

3x + 3

(A) $\frac{5}{2}x^2 + 19x + 12$

(B) $5x^2 + 19x + 6$

(C) $5x^2 + 19x - 6$

(D) $\frac{5}{2}x^2 + \frac{19}{2}x + 6$

411. Identify the vertex of the parabola.

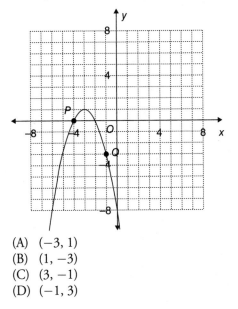

(A) $(-3, 1)$
(B) $(1, -3)$
(C) $(3, -1)$
(D) $(-1, 3)$

412. Write the equation of the parabola in vertex form given: vertex $(0, 3)$, point $(-4, -45)$.

(A) $y = -4x^2 + 3$
(B) $y = -3x^2 + 3$
(C) $y = -45x^2 - 3$
(D) $y = -3x^2 - 3$

413. Which of the following is equal to $(2x - 9)^2$?

(A) $x^2 - 18x - 81$
(B) $4x^2 + 36x + 81$
(C) $4x^2 - 36x + 81$
(D) $4x^2 + 36x - 81$

414. What are the coordinates of the vertex of the graph $y = (x - 6)(x + 5)$?

(A) $\left(-\dfrac{1}{2}, -\dfrac{25}{2}\right)$

(B) $\left(\dfrac{1}{2}, -\dfrac{121}{4}\right)$

(C) $(2, -28)$

(D) $\left(-\dfrac{1}{2}, \dfrac{-96}{4}\right)$

415. Which of the following is the solution for the proportion $\dfrac{4}{y+9} = \dfrac{6}{y-7}$?

    (A) -82

    (B) -41

    (C) -13

    (D) 41

416. What is the simplified form of the expression $\dfrac{x^3 - 10x^2 + 9x}{x^2 + 5x - 6}$?

    (A) $\dfrac{x-9}{x+6}$

    (B) $\dfrac{x(x-9)}{x+6}$

    (C) $\dfrac{x}{x+6}$

    (D) $\dfrac{x}{(x-1)(x+6)}$

417. Simplify the expression $\dfrac{9x^2}{4x} * \dfrac{16x^3}{x^5}$.

    (A) 36

    (B) $36x$

    (C) $\dfrac{9}{x}$

    (D) $\dfrac{36}{x}$

418. Factor the expression $-15x^2 - 21x$.

    (A) $x(-15x - 21)$

    (B) $-15x(x + 7)$

    (C) $-3x(5x + 7)$

    (D) $5x(x - 3 + 7)$

419. Which of the following represents the equation $f(x) = (x-3)^2 + 3x - 3$?

(A)

(B)

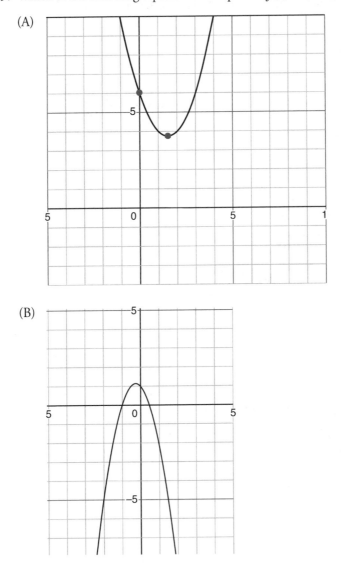

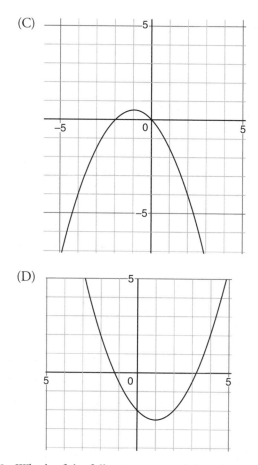

(C)

(D)

420. Which of the following is one of the solutions for the equation $x^2 - 2x = 120$?

(A) -12
(B) -10
(C) 10
(D) 20

421. Which is the graph of $y = (x-2)^2 + 4$?

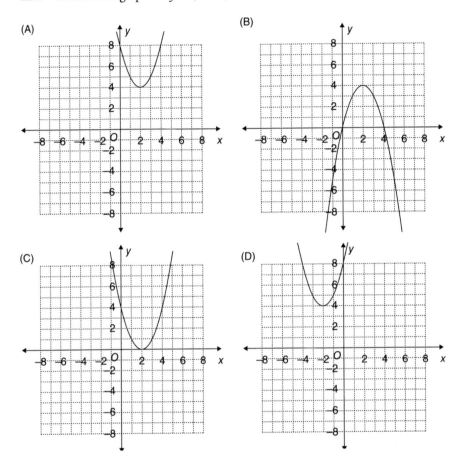

422. Simplify $\sqrt{-63}$ using the imaginary number i.
Note $i = \sqrt{-1}$.

(A) $3\sqrt{-7}$

(B) $i\sqrt{63}$

(C) $-3\sqrt{7}$

(D) $3i\sqrt{7}$

423. Write an equation for the parabola whose vertex is at (3, 6) and which passes through point (4, 4).

(A) $y = -2(x+3)^2 - 6$

(B) $y = (x+3)^2 - 6$

(C) $y = 2(x-3)^2 + 6$

(D) $y = -2(x-3)^2 + 6$

424. Factor the expression $x^2 + 11x + 28$.

(A) $(x+7)(x+4)$

(B) $(x+7)(x-4)$

(C) $(x+4)(x-7)$

(D) $(x-4)(x-7)$

425. Solve the quadratic equation $x^2 + 10x + 22 = 0$ by completing the square.

(A) $5 \pm 2\sqrt{7}$

(B) $-5 \pm \sqrt{3}$

(C) $100 \pm \sqrt{3}$

(D) $-10 \pm 2\sqrt{7}$

426. The function $y = -16t^2 + 248$ models the height y in feet of a stone t seconds after it is dropped from the edge of a vertical cliff. How long will it take the stone to hit the ground? Round to the nearest hundredth of a second.

(A) 0.25 seconds

(B) 3.94 seconds

(C) 5.57 seconds

(D) 7.87 seconds

427. Which of the following is a possible solution for the equation

$$\frac{x^2 + 6x + 9}{3} \times \frac{2}{x+3} = 3?$$

(A) $\dfrac{1}{2}$

(B) $\dfrac{5}{6}$

(C) $\dfrac{3}{2}$

(D) $\sqrt{6}$

428. Which of the following quadratics have the solution $x = -5$ and $x = -1$?

(A) $x^2 + 4x - 5 = 0$

(B) $x^2 - 4x - 5 = 0$

(C) $x^2 - 6x - 5 = 0$

(D) $x^2 + 6x + 5 = 0$

429. What is the simplified form of the expression $\dfrac{x^2 - 64}{3x^2} \div (x - 8)$?

(A) $\dfrac{x + 8}{3x^2}$

(B) $\dfrac{x - 8}{3x^2}$

(C) $\dfrac{1}{3x^2}$

(D) $\dfrac{x^3 - 512}{3x}$

430. What is $x^2 + 24x - 3$ divided by $x - 4$?

(A) $\dfrac{x + 28}{x - 4} + 109$

(B) $\dfrac{x - 4}{x + 28} + 109$

(C) $x + 28 + \dfrac{109}{x - 4}$

(D) $\dfrac{x - 4}{x + 28}$

431. Solve by factoring $4x^2 + 10x - 24 = 0$

(A) $\dfrac{3}{2}, -1$

(B) $4, -\dfrac{3}{2}$

(C) $4, -1$

(D) $-4, 4$

432. What is the value of $f(x) = \dfrac{x\sqrt{x^2 - 1}}{x^2 - 8}$ when $x = 8$?

(A) $\dfrac{3\sqrt{7}}{7}$

(B) $\dfrac{7}{8}$

(C) $\dfrac{\sqrt{7}}{3}$

(D) $\dfrac{8}{9}$

433. Evaluate the expression $5\sqrt{7} + \sqrt{448} + \sqrt{175} - \sqrt{63}$.

(A) $15\sqrt{7}$
(B) $16\sqrt{7}$
(C) $18\sqrt{7}$
(D) $20\sqrt{7}$

434. Which one of the following is the simplified expression of $(3 - \sqrt{6})^2$?

(A) $9 - 5\sqrt{6}$
(B) $3 - 6\sqrt{6}$
(C) $15 - 6\sqrt{6}$
(D) None of these

435. Factor the expression $6x^2 - 4x + 8$.

(A) $6x(3x - 2)$
(B) $3(2x^2 - 4x + 8)$
(C) $6x^2 - 4x + 8$
(D) $2(3x^2 - 2x + 4)$

436. If $2x - y = 8$, then what is the value of $\dfrac{9^x}{3^y}$?

(A) 2^3
(B) 3^4
(C) 4^5
(D) 3^8

437. A manufacturer determines that the number of drills it can sell is given by the formula $D = -4p^2 + 152p - 270$, where p is the price of the drills in dollars. At what price will the manufacturer sell the maximum number of drills?

    (A) $19
    (B) $22
    (C) $20
    (D) $40

438. What is the solution of the system of linear equations?

$$\frac{4}{5}x + \frac{1}{2}y = 16$$

$$x + y = 24$$

    (A) (8, 16)

    (B) (10. 14)

    (C) $\left(\dfrac{40}{3}, \dfrac{32}{3}\right)$

    (D) $\left(\dfrac{41}{4}, \dfrac{55}{4}\right)$

439. Expand and simplify $(2x - 1)(x + 3)$.

    (A) $2x^2 + x - 3$
    (B) $2x^2 + 5x - 3$
    (C) $2x^2 - 7x + 3$
    (D) $2x^2 - 5x - 3$

440. Factor completely: $4x^2 - 4x + 1$.

    (A) $(4x - 1)(x + 1)$
    (B) $(2x - 1)(2x + 1)$
    (C) $(4x + 1)(x - 1)$
    (D) $(2x - 1)^2$

441. Which equation of a parabola has zeros at -1 and 2?

    (A) $y = (x - 1)(x + 2)$
    (B) $(x + 1) = (x - 2)$
    (C) $(x - 1) = (x + 2)$
    (D) $y = (x + 1)(x - 2)$

442. Which equation has roots -2 and 1?

    (A) $(x+1)=(x-2)$

    (B) $(x-1)=(x+2)$

    (C) $y=x^2+x-2$

    (D) $y=x^2-x-2$

443. Solve for x.

$$18-\frac{(3x)^{\frac{1}{2}}}{2}=15$$

444. Which of the following are solutions to the quadratic equation $(x-2)^2=\dfrac{16}{25}$?

    (A) $x=\pm\sqrt{\dfrac{4}{5}}$

    (B) $x=-\dfrac{4}{5},\ x=\dfrac{4}{5}$

    (C) $x=\dfrac{6}{5},\ x=\dfrac{14}{5}$

    (D) $x=\dfrac{14}{5},\ x=-\dfrac{14}{5}$

Additional Topics in Math

This section covers the remaining topics covered on the SAT. These include geometry, trigonometry, and complex numbers. The test provides formulas for areas and volumes of most regular shapes.

Topics

- Volume and area of regular shapes and circles
- Theorems related to angles, arcs, and trigonometry functions
- Circle theorems and equations
- Word problems involving geometry and complex numbers

Skills

- Apply formulas to determine area and volume.
- Apply properties of right triangles to determine angle measures or side length.
- Apply properties of a circle to determine arc length and area.
- Use trigonometry formulas for sine, cosine, and tangent to determine measurements.

Need to Know

- Congruence
- Similarity
- Trigonometry formulas
  - $\sin(x)$ = Measure of the opposite side to the angle / Measure of the hypotenuse
  - $\cos(x)$ = Measure of the adjacent side to the angle / Measure of the hypotenuse
  - $\tan(x)$ = Measure of the opposite side to the angle / Measure of the adjacent side to the angle

Answer Questions 445–460 without a calculator.

445. Triangle *ABC* shown is a right triangle such that angle *ABC* has a measure of 55 degrees. What is the measure of angle *BCD*, in degrees?

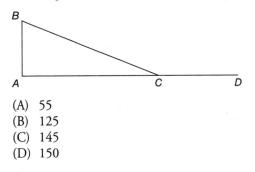

    (A) 55
    (B) 125
    (C) 145
    (D) 150

446. In square units, what is the area of the following figure?

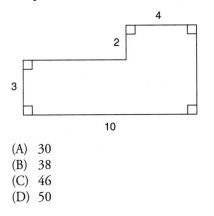

    (A) 30
    (B) 38
    (C) 46
    (D) 50

447. What is the area of a circle inscribed in a square with sides of length 6?

    (A) 6π
    (B) 9π
    (C) 12π
    (D) 18π

448. A ladder of length 12 feet is placed against a building. If the top of the ladder reaches a height of *x* feet, which of the following represents the distance from the bottom of the ladder to the building in terms of *x*?

    (A) $\sqrt{x^2 - 144}$
    (B) $\sqrt{144 - x^2}$
    (C) $\sqrt{12 + x^2}$
    (D) $x + 12$

449. In the following figure, triangle *ABC* is an equilateral triangle and point *M* is the midpoint of $\overline{AC}$. If the length of side *BC* is 4, what is the perimeter of triangle *ABM*?

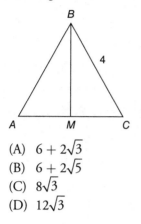

(A) $6 + 2\sqrt{3}$
(B) $6 + 2\sqrt{5}$
(C) $8\sqrt{3}$
(D) $12\sqrt{3}$

450. What is the value of *x* in the following figure?

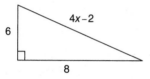

451. The length of a rectangle is six times as large as its width. If its perimeter is 42 units, what is its area in square units?

452. In the following figure, triangle *ABC* is an isosceles triangle with *AC = BC*. Which of the following is the value of angle *DCE* in degrees?

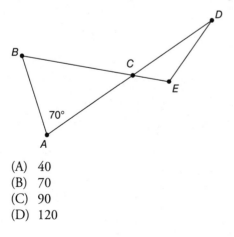

(A) 40
(B) 70
(C) 90
(D) 120

453. If the length of one side of an equilateral triangle is z, which of the following represents the perimeter of the triangle in terms of z?

(A) $\dfrac{z}{2}$

(B) $3z$

(C) $4z$

(D) z^3

454. If $\sin \alpha = \dfrac{1}{3}$ and $\tan \alpha = \dfrac{5}{12}$, then what is the value of $\cos \alpha$?

(A) $\dfrac{1}{12}$

(B) $\dfrac{2}{5}$

(C) $\dfrac{5}{12}$

(D) $\dfrac{4}{5}$

455. In the following figure, $\overline{AC}$, $\overline{CD}$, and $\overline{DA}$ have the same lengths and $\overline{AC}$ is the diameter of the half circle centered at point B. If the length of $\overline{CD}$ is x, which of the following represents the area of the half circle in terms of x?

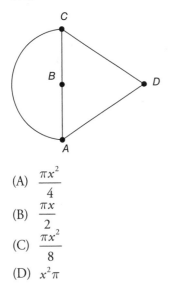

(A) $\dfrac{\pi x^2}{4}$

(B) $\dfrac{\pi x}{2}$

(C) $\dfrac{\pi x^2}{8}$

(D) $x^2 \pi$

456. In the following rectangle *ABCD*, the shortest distance between points *A* and *C* is *d*. Which of the following is the ratio between *d* and $x^2 + y^2$?

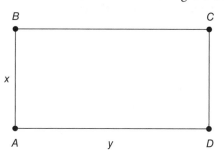

457. The diameter of circle 1 is *m*, and the diameter of circle 2 is 4*m*. How many times larger is the area of circle 2 than the area of circle 1?

(A) 4
(B) 8
(C) 16
(D) 32

458. The length of one side of a square is equal to the diameter of a circle. Which of the following statements must be true?

I. The area of the square is larger than the area of the circle.
II. The perimeter of the square is smaller than the circumference of the circle.
III. The radius of the circle is the same as the perimeter of the square.

(A) I only
(B) II only
(C) III only
(D) I and II only

459. In the following figure, AOB is a segment of the circle centered at O with a radius of 5. If the angle AOB has a measure of 40 degrees, what is the perimeter of the segment AOB outlined with a solid line?

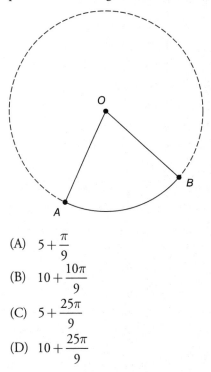

(A) $5 + \dfrac{\pi}{9}$

(B) $10 + \dfrac{10\pi}{9}$

(C) $5 + \dfrac{25\pi}{9}$

(D) $10 + \dfrac{25\pi}{9}$

Questions 460–500 should be answered without a calculator.

460. A rectangular storage container is completely filled with 40 boxes. Each box measures 2 inches tall, 3 inches wide, and 10 inches long. What is the volume of the storage container in cubic inches?

(A) 400
(B) 640
(C) 1800
(D) 2400

461. In the following figure, square $ABCD$ is inscribed in the circle with center O. If the length of $\overline{AB}$ is 8 and the length of $\overline{PQ}$ is 12, what is the area of the shaded region?

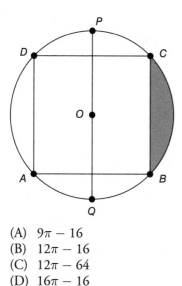

(A) $9\pi - 16$
(B) $12\pi - 16$
(C) $12\pi - 64$
(D) $16\pi - 16$

462. In the following figure, there are four angles marked as $a = 70$ degrees, $b = 80$ degrees, angle c, and exterior angle $\frac{3}{2}c$. What is the value of c, in degrees?

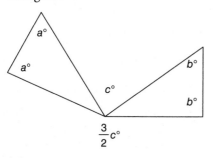

(A) 90
(B) 120
(C) 300
(D) 440

463. The area of triangle ABC is twice the area of triangle DEF. The height of triangle ABC is 4, and the height of triangle DEF is 3. If b_1 is the length of the base of triangle ABC and b_2 is the length of the base of triangle DEF, what is the value of $\frac{b_1}{b_2}$?

464. Rectangle 1 has sides of length k and $2k$, while rectangle 2 has sides of length k and $6k$. If k is an integer, how many times larger is the area of rectangle 2 than the area of rectangle 1?

(A) 3
(B) 4
(C) 6
(D) 8

465. If $0° < x° < 90°$ and $\sin x = \dfrac{1}{2}$, then $\cos x = ?$

(A) $\dfrac{1}{2}$

(B) $\dfrac{\sqrt{3}}{2}$

(C) $\dfrac{\sqrt{3}}{3}$

(D) 2

466. The half circles in the following figure are centered at points B and D. If the length of line segment $\overline{AB}$ is 4 and the total area of the figure is 40π, what is the length of $\overline{AE}$?

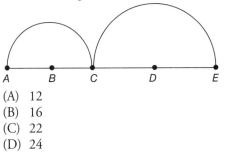

(A) 12
(B) 16
(C) 22
(D) 24

467. In the following figure, triangles ABC and PQR are equilateral, the length of $\overline{AB}$ is 4, and the length of $\overline{PQ}$ is 2. If M is the midpoint of line segments $\overline{AC}$ and $\overline{PR}$, what is the perimeter of the shaded figure?

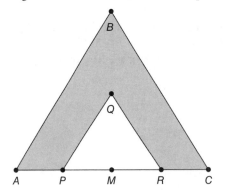

(A) 10
(B) 12
(C) 14
(D) 16

468. In the following figure, triangle *ABC* is an equilateral triangle. Which of the following is the perimeter of the right triangle *ABD* in terms of *x*?

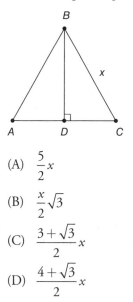

(A) $\dfrac{5}{2}x$

(B) $\dfrac{x}{2}\sqrt{3}$

(C) $\dfrac{3+\sqrt{3}}{2}x$

(D) $\dfrac{4+\sqrt{3}}{2}x$

469. A rectangular prism has a height of *h* and a width of *w*. If the volume of the prism is $\dfrac{19}{2}$, then which of the following represents the length of the prism in terms of *h* and *w*?

(A) $\dfrac{19}{2wh}$

(B) $\dfrac{19wh}{2}$

(C) $wh\sqrt{\dfrac{19}{2}}$

(D) $\dfrac{19}{2}-wh$

470. If $\sin \alpha = \dfrac{12}{13}$, and $\cos \alpha = \dfrac{5}{13}$, then $\tan \alpha =$

(A) $\dfrac{5}{12}$

(B) $\dfrac{7}{13}$

(C) $\dfrac{12}{5}$

(D) $\dfrac{13}{5}$

471. One interior angle of a parallelogram has a measure of 80 degrees. If the remaining angles have measures $x°$, $y°$, and $z°$, what is the value of $x + y + z$ in degrees?

(A) 100
(B) 180
(C) 240
(D) 280

472. It requires 4 gallons of paint to cover 10 square meters of area. If five sides of a cube with a volume of 27 cubic meters are to be painted, how many gallons of paint will be required?

(A) 5
(B) 18
(C) 20
(D) 22

473. A rectangle has a width of 2 centimeters. When the rectangle's length is increased by 8 and the width remains the same, its area is increased by 50%. What is the length of the original rectangle?

474. Find $\cos A$ in the following figure.

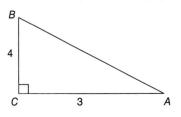

(A) 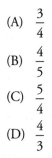 $\dfrac{3}{4}$

(B) $\dfrac{4}{5}$

(C) $\dfrac{5}{4}$

(D) $\dfrac{4}{3}$

475. In the following figure, *ABCH*, *CDGH*, and *GDEF* are congruent squares and the half circles have diameters $\overline{BC}$ and $\overline{DE}$. If $\overline{AB}$ has a length of 2 centimeters, what is the length of the path outlined by the solid line rounded to the nearest centimeter?

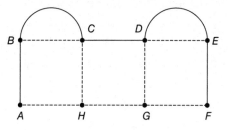

476. The total perimeter of two separate equilateral triangles with sides of length *a* and *b*, respectively, is 72. If *a* is one-fifth as large as *b*, what is the value of *b*?

477. The following figure has two horizontal lines that are parallel. What is the value of $x + y$?

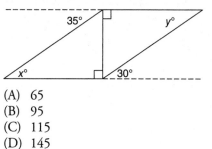

(A) 65
(B) 95
(C) 115
(D) 145

478. What is the sine of angle $\angle A$?

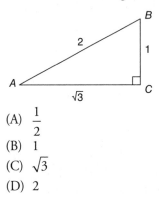

(A) $\dfrac{1}{2}$

(B) 1

(C) $\sqrt{3}$

(D) 2

479. What is the area of the shaded region in the following figure?

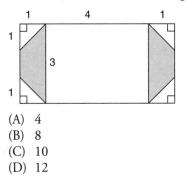

(A) 4

(B) 8

(C) 10

(D) 12

480. In an equilateral triangle ABC, points D, E, and F are the midpoints of $\overline{AB}$, $\overline{BC}$, and $\overline{AC}$, respectively. If AD has a length of 2, what is the area of triangle DEF?

(A) $\dfrac{\sqrt{3}}{4}$

(B) $\dfrac{\sqrt{3}}{2}$

(C) $\sqrt{3}$

(D) $4\sqrt{3}$

481. In the following figure, y and z lie along the same line. What is the value of z in terms of x?

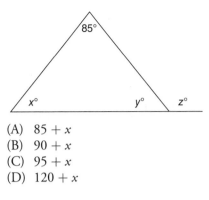

- (A) $85 + x$
- (B) $90 + x$
- (C) $95 + x$
- (D) $120 + x$

482. In the following figure, $ABCE$ is a square and ABD is a right triangle. What is the value of x?

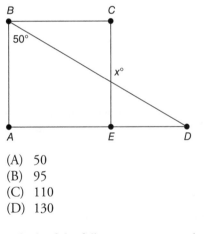

- (A) 50
- (B) 95
- (C) 110
- (D) 130

483. Which of the following represents the area of a right triangle whose interior angles measure $45°$, $45°$, and $90°$ and whose hypotenuse has a length of $3\sqrt{2}$?

- (A) $\dfrac{3}{2}$
- (B) $\dfrac{3\sqrt{2}}{2}$
- (C) $\dfrac{9}{2}$
- (D) $9\sqrt{2}$

484. The base of a 10-meter-tall cylindrical container is a circle with a radius of 4 meters. If the container is completely filled, how many cubic meters of water can it hold?

(A) 40π
(B) 80π
(C) 160π
(D) 210π

485. What is the approximate length of side $\overline{AB}$?

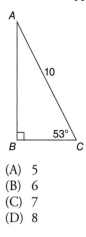

(A) 5
(B) 6
(C) 7
(D) 8

486. The following figure consists of two concentric circles centered at point A with radii of 5 and 9, respectively. What is the area of the shaded region?

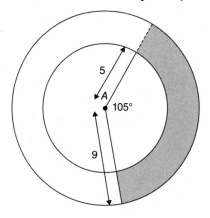

(A) $\dfrac{\pi}{3}$

(B) $\dfrac{4\pi}{3}$

(C) $\dfrac{14\pi}{3}$

(D) $\dfrac{49\pi}{3}$

487. In the following figure, *ABCD* is a parallelogram and *DCE* is a triangle. If $y = 55$, what is the value of *x*?

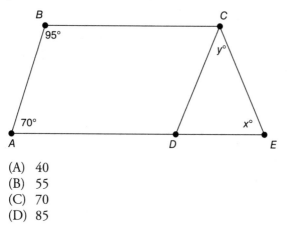

(A) 40
(B) 55
(C) 70
(D) 85

488. Which of the following represents the perimeter of a square that has an area of x^2?

(A) $\dfrac{1}{2}x$

(B) $2x$

(C) $3x$

(D) $4x$

489. In the following figure, *ABCD* is a single face of a cube, and the length of the diagonal $\overline{BD}$ is *x*. Which of the following represents the volume of the cube in terms of *x*?

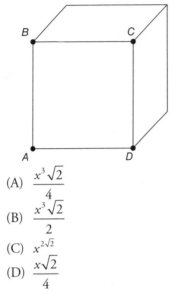

(A) $\dfrac{x^3 \sqrt{2}}{4}$

(B) $\dfrac{x^3 \sqrt{2}}{2}$

(C) $x^{2\sqrt{2}}$

(D) $\dfrac{x\sqrt{2}}{4}$

490. When the radius of a circle is halved, the area of the new circle is 16π. What is the radius of the original circle?

491. In the following figure, *ABD* is a quarter circle with a radius of 10. What is the area of the shaded region?

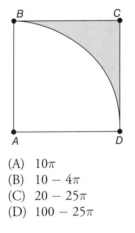

(A) 10π

(B) $10 - 4\pi$

(C) $20 - 25\pi$

(D) $100 - 25\pi$

492. If the points A, B, C, D, E, and F form a hexagon and each point is connected to every other point by a line segment, how many line segments will contain point A?

(A) 2

(B) 4

(C) 5

(D) 6

493. What is the volume of a cube with a surface area of 294?

494. In the right triangle shown, the length of $\overline{AB}$ is 13 units and the length of $\overline{CB}$ is 12 units. What is the tangent of $\angle A$?

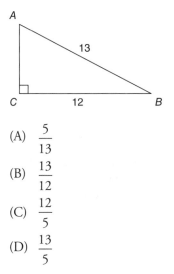

(A) $\dfrac{5}{13}$

(B) $\dfrac{13}{12}$

(C) $\dfrac{12}{5}$

(D) $\dfrac{13}{5}$

495. In the following figure, the half circles centered at points B and D have radii of x and $2x$, respectively. Which of the following represents the length of the path denoted by the solid line in terms of x?

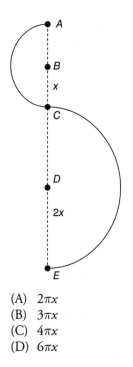

(A) $2\pi x$
(B) $3\pi x$
(C) $4\pi x$
(D) $6\pi x$

496. A person had a rectangular-shaped garden with sides of lengths 16 feet and 9 feet. The garden was changed into a square design with the same area as the original rectangular-shaped garden. How many feet in length are each of the sides of the new square-shaped garden?

(A) 7
(B) 9
(C) 12
(D) $5\sqrt{7}$

497. What is the smallest positive value for x where $y = \sin 2x$ reaches its maximum?

(A) $\dfrac{\pi}{4}$

(B) π

(C) $\dfrac{3\pi}{2}$

(D) $\dfrac{2\pi}{3}$

498. Two rectangular prisms A and B have the same width and height. If the length of prism A is a third of that of prism B, then the ratio of the volume of A to the volume of B is

(A) 1:3
(B) 1:6
(C) 1:9
(D) 1:12

499. The circumference of a circle is C and the perimeter of a square is P such that $P = \dfrac{C}{\pi}$. If the area of the circle is A_c and the area of the square is A_s, then $A_s =$

(A) A_c

(B) $\dfrac{A_c}{\pi}$

(C) $\dfrac{A_c}{3\pi}$

(D) $\dfrac{A_c}{4\pi}$

500. If the perimeter of rectangle $ABCD$ in the following figure is 18, what is the length of $\overline{BD}$?

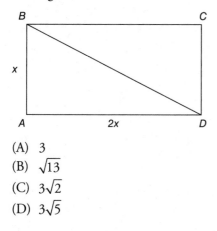

(A) 3
(B) $\sqrt{13}$
(C) $3\sqrt{2}$
(D) $3\sqrt{5}$

ANSWERS

Section 1

1. **(A)** $21-3=18$, so j must be a number that fits evenly into 18: $\dfrac{21}{6}=3R3$; therefore, $j=6$ and it is less than 9 as required. $\dfrac{30}{6}=5R0$.

2. **(B)** $m-n=\left(3*8^{-2}\right)-\left(5*8^{-2}\right)=\dfrac{3}{8^2}-\dfrac{5}{8^2}=\dfrac{-2}{64}=-\dfrac{1}{32}$

3. **(C)** The following are answers worked out, with $x=-1$ plugged in the third step:

   (A) $-x^{-1}=\dfrac{-1}{x^1}=\dfrac{-1}{(-1)^1}=1$

   (B) $x^{-2}=\dfrac{1}{x^2}=\dfrac{1}{(-1)^2}=\dfrac{1}{1}=1$

   (C) $-2x^{-2}=\dfrac{-2}{x^2}=\dfrac{-2}{(-1)^2}=\dfrac{-2}{1}=-2$

   (D) $2x^{-2}=\dfrac{2}{x^2}=\dfrac{2}{(-1)^2}=\dfrac{2}{1}=2$

   The smallest value is -2.

4. **(C)** Of the 19 students in history, 7 are also in physics; therefore, 12 history students are only enrolled in history. Of the 24 students in physics, 7 are also enrolled in history; therefore 17 are only enrolled in physics. $12+17=29$ students who are enrolled in only one of the two courses.

5. **(A)** x must be evenly divisible by 3, 4, and 11. Thus, x must be divisible by the product of any of these numbers. Since $3*4=12$, and 12 is evenly divisible by 6, then x is a multiple of 6. (Note: If you take $3*4*11=132$, you'll see that 8, 16, and 47 do not divide evenly into this product.)

6. **(A)**

   $$n^4=144$$
   $$(n^2)^2=144$$
   $$\sqrt{(n^2)^2}=\sqrt{144}$$
   $$n^2=12$$

7. **(D)**

   I. $14a = b^2c^6 \rightarrow a = \dfrac{b^2c^6}{14} = \dfrac{(bc^3)^2}{14}$

   II. $14a = b^2c^6 \rightarrow 14a = (bc^3)^2$

   III. $\dfrac{14a = b^2c^6}{14b^2} \rightarrow \dfrac{a}{b^2} = \dfrac{c^6}{14} \rightarrow ab^{-2} = \dfrac{c^6}{14}$

   Only I and III match the original algebraic expression.

8. **(B)** Only choices A and B will be negative, so they may both qualify for the smallest value. Because $p > n$, then mp will be more negative than mn.

9. **(B)** $\dfrac{m}{n} = \dfrac{\left(\dfrac{p}{q}\right)^2}{\left(\dfrac{q}{p}\right)^{-2}} = \left(\dfrac{p}{q}\right)^2\left(\dfrac{q}{p}\right)^2 = \left(\dfrac{pq}{pq}\right)^2 = (1)^2 = 1$

10. (Grid-in answer $= 1$) Any odd integer over 10 will work for this. Using 11 as the odd integer, $\dfrac{11}{2} = 5R1$. So the remainder is 1.

11. **(D)** $jk = \left(\dfrac{1}{4^{-2}}\right)\left(\dfrac{3}{2^{-1}}\right) = (4^2)(3)(2^1) = (16)(3)(2) = 96$

12. **(C)** $\dfrac{-1}{a^3}$ must be positive because the cube of a negative number is always negative.

   $a + 10$ could be positive if $-10 < a < 0$. $2a^{-1} = \dfrac{2}{a}$ and will *always* be negative since a is negative, so this is the only choice that fits the criteria.

13. **(A)** $\left(\dfrac{2}{3}m^3n^{\frac{1}{2}}\right)^2 = \left(\dfrac{2}{3}\right)^2(m^3)^2\left(n^{\frac{1}{2}}\right)^2 = \dfrac{2^2}{3^2}m^6n = \dfrac{4}{9}m^6n$

14. (Grid-in answer) To calculate this, we need to do the following:

   $3^{4*2} = (3)^{3*3b}$
   $3^8 = 3^{9b}$
   $8 = 9b$
   $b = \dfrac{8}{9}$

15. **(A)** The square of a number is always positive:

$$|-(-x)^2| = 9$$
$$|-x^2| = 9$$
$$x^2 = 9$$
$$x = \pm 3$$

16. **(B)** $\dfrac{x^2}{2} + x$ is the first equation divided by 6. This means that its value will be $\dfrac{18}{6} = 3$.

17. **(C)** Let x be the smaller integer:

$$x + (x+1) = 75$$
$$x + x = 75 - 1$$
$$2x = 74$$
$$x = \frac{74}{2} = 37$$

18. **(C)** $4ab = 24$

$$ab = \frac{24}{4} = 6$$
$$(2ab)^2 = 4(ab)^2 = 4(6)^2 = 144$$

19. **(A)** "Difference" means subtract $(a - b)$. "7 less than the sum (addition) of the first two numbers" $= (a + b) - 7$.

20. **(D)** $3x^2 = 2a$ (will use to substitute)

$$(3x - a)(3x + a) = 9x^2 - a^2$$
$$9x^2 - a^2 = 3(3x^2) - a^2 = 3(2a) - a^2 = 6a - a^2$$

21. **(C)** If Bobby is 6 years older than Gina, who is 4 years older than Ann, then Bobby must be 10 years older than Ann.

22. **(B)** If the revenue of company C is the square root of the revenue of company B, then the revenue of company B is the square root of $2,500, which is 50. The revenue of company A is three times that value, which is $150.

23. (D) Amount left = Total budget − Total spent

Total budget = x

Total spent = k(dollars) * n(days)

Amount left = $x - kn$

24. (C) First 3 months: $15 * 3$(months) = $45

Last 6 months: $10 * 6$(months) = $60

Total = $45 + $60 = $105

25. (Grid-in answer = 132)

Known: $x + y = 28$ and $x - y = 16$.

Solve for x: $x = 28 - y$

Plug into $x - y = 16$:

$28 - y - y = 16$

$12 = 2y$

$y = 6$ and $x = 28 - 6 = 22$

Find product: $x * y = 22 * 6 = 132$

26. (B) We can input the value of y, which leads us to the equation $8x^2 = 128$. This means that when we divide the entire equation by 8, we can simplify it to $x^2 = 16$. Therefore, the highest possible value to satisfy this equation would be 4.

27. (C) If 3 is the first value, then the first 10 values in the series are 3, 4, 5, 7, 11, 19, 35, 67, 131, and 259. Therefore, the correct answer choice is (C).

28. (B) Test each inequality:

$(a) -5 < 2(-3) < 7$: *False*

$(b) -5 < 2(-2) < 7$: *True*

$(c) -5 < 2(4) < 7$: *False*

$(d) -5 < 2(7) < 7$: *False*

29. (C) Known: $a = 2x + 4y$ and $b = x + 2y$.

$$\frac{a}{b} = \frac{2x + 4y}{x + 2y} = \frac{2(x + 2y)}{(x + 2y)} = 2$$

a is 2 times larger than b.

30. (D) $x \oplus y = \dfrac{x + y^2}{x}$

$$(2xy) \oplus (4xy) = \frac{(2xy) + (4xy)^2}{(2xy)} = \frac{(2xy) + (16x^2y^2)}{(2xy)} = 1 + 8xy$$

31. (B) If 15 is the final value of the series, then the series will be 15, 13, 11, 9, 7, and 5. The second value is 7.

32. (A) Hourly wage $= (11.50 + 1.25) = 12.75$

Weekly wage $= 12.75 * h$

33. (A) $-\dfrac{2}{3}a \geq 1$

$\dfrac{2}{3}a \leq -1$

$a \leq -\dfrac{3}{2}$

34. (B) This can be solved through calculation. By multiplying the entire equation by 15 (5×3), we get the following:

$9x + 18 = 10x + 25$

$9x + 18 - 18 = 10x + 25 - 18$

$9x = 10x + 7$

$9x - 10x = 10x - 10x + 7$

$-x = 7$

$x = -7$

35. (A) None of the spice mixture will be fresh after 4 months because it only stays fresh for 3 months.

36. (C) The point of intercept is calculated by making the two equations equal each other. After solving $3x - 2 = 2x + 4$, you get $x = 6$. Then, this value can be placed into either equation to infer that $y = 3 * 6 - 2 = 16$.

37. (A) A line will be perpendicular to another if the value of their slopes, when multiplied, results in –1. The correct response is (A) because multiplying $-\dfrac{1}{2}$ by 2 results in –1.

38. (A) If a line is perpendicular to another, then the value of the multiplication of the two slopes needs to be –1. For this condition to be achieved, the value of the slope of the perpendicular line should be –4.

Then, we can use the following form to find the final equation:

$y - y_1 = m(x - x_1)$, where we are aware of the value of the slope (m) and the point through which the line has to go through. By inputting these values, we can infer the following:

$y - 5 = -4(x - 2)$

$y - 5 = -4x + 8$

Finally, we can utilize the distributive property to add 5 to both sides, resulting in

$y = -4x + 13$

39. **(D)** $y = mx$ at point $(2, 8)$
$$8 = 2x$$
$$x = \frac{8}{2} = 4$$

40. **(A)** The only condition for parallel lines is identical slope. If line ℓ and line m are parallel, they must have the same slope (with the same sign). If line ℓ has a negative slope, line m must also; therefore, only I is true. The lines can cross the x-axis and y-axis at any value, positive or negative.

41. **(B)** The line crosses the y-axis and the y-intercept of the equation (b in the equation $y = mx + b$). The y-intercept of $y = -4x - 9$ is -9.

42. **(C)** Given the points $(-1, 2)$ and $(1, 6)$, find the equation:
$$m(\text{slope}) = \frac{\Delta y}{\Delta x} = \frac{6-2}{1-(-1)} = 2$$
$$y = 2x + b \text{ [plug in point } (-1, 2)]$$
$$2 = 2(-1) + b$$
$$b = 4$$
Equation: $y = 2x + 4$, when x is 0 then $y = 4$.

43. **(D)** Assume Chuck's house is the orgin $(0, 0)$.
Carly's house is a total of five blocks north and two blocks east $(2, 5)$.
Use the distance equation with these two points:
$$\sqrt{(x_2 - x_1)^2 + (y_2 - y_1)^2} = \sqrt{(2-0)^2 + (5-0)^2} = \sqrt{4 + 25} = \sqrt{29}$$

44. **(B)** Known: slope $= -3$, y-intercept $= 6$.
Write as equation: $y = (-3)x + 6$
Find x when y is 0: $0 = (-3)x + 6$
$(-3)x = -6$
$x = 2$

45. **(B)** The graph must start with an upward slope, be a flat line for a time with a slope of 0, and then continue up with a slope less steep than the original. Only graph B matches this.

46. **(A)** If the line passes through the x-axis at that point, then this means that the value of y is equal to 0. This can be included in the equation as follows:
$$0 = 2x + 4$$
$$-2x = 4$$
$$x = -2$$
Then, the correct coordinates are $(-2, 0)$.

47. (Grid-in answer $= 50$)

The angle between BC and BA is 180 degrees because it is a straight line.

$180 - 30 = 150$ degrees

$3x = 150$ $\therefore$ $x = \dfrac{150}{3} = 50$

48. (C) $m = \left(\dfrac{\text{rise}}{\text{run}}\right) = \dfrac{(y_2 - y_1)}{(x_2 - x_1)} = \dfrac{(t+9)-(t+4)}{(t+7)-t} = \dfrac{5}{7}$

49. (A) Two lines will be parallel if the value of their slope is identical. In the case of (I), the slope is identical. In the case of (III), the lines are perpendicular rather than parallel.

50. (A) Perpendicular lines have slopes that are negative reciprocals of each other. For this

example, $b = -\dfrac{1}{a}$ $\therefore$ $a * b = a * -\dfrac{1}{a} = -1$

51. (C) The only information that is really necessary is the value of the intercept and the first equation. By inputting the value for x and y, we can infer that

$-7 = -4t + 1$

$4t = 8$

$t = 2$

52. (A) All the other answer choices would not pass through $(0, 5)$. Answer choice (C) would pass through $(0, -5)$.

53. (C) When reflecting over the line $y = x$, the x- and y-coordinates of a point will switch.

54. (B) $m = \left(\dfrac{\text{Rise}}{\text{Run}}\right) = \dfrac{(y_2 - y_1)}{(x_2 - x_1)} = \dfrac{(2y - y)}{(2x - x)} = \dfrac{y}{x}$

55. (A) Known: $2xy = 7(m + n)$ and $2(m + n) = 8$.

$2(2xy) = 2 * [7(m + n)]$

$4xy = 7[2(m + n)] = 7(8)$

$xy = \dfrac{7(8)}{4} = 14$

$x = \dfrac{14}{y}$

56. (B) $-3x + 2 < -2x + 4$

$-3x + 2 - 4 < -2x$

$2 - 4 < -2x + 3x$

$-2 < x \text{ or } x > -2$

57. (C) Let L be the cost of a large shirt and S be the cost of a small.

Known: $14L + 10S = 248$ and $6L + 2S = 88$.

Solve $6L + 2S = 88$ for S: $2S = 88 - 6L$ ∴ $S = 44 - 3L$

Plug S back into the first equation: $14L + 10S = 248$

$14L + 10(44 - 3L) = 248$

$14L + 440 - 30L = 248$

$-16L = -192$ ∴ $L = \dfrac{-192}{-16} = 12$

Plug L into the second equation: $6L + 2S = 88$

$6*12 + 2S = 88$ ∴ $S = \dfrac{88 - (6*12)}{2} = 8$

58. (D) $x^2 = 9$ and $x > 0$ ∴ $x = 3$

$xy = 12 = 3y$ ∴ $y = \dfrac{12}{3} = 4$

$(x - 2y)^2 = [3 - 2(4)]^2 = (-5)^2 = 25$

59. (B) Known: $m = 3n$ and $k = 2n$.

$n = \dfrac{m}{3}$ and $k = 2 * \dfrac{m}{3} = \dfrac{2m}{3}$

60. (Grid-in answer $= 2$)

$(a - b)*(a + b) = a^2 - b^2 = 6$

$a^2 = 8$

$8 - b^2 = 6$ ∴ $b^2 = 2$

61. (B) Known: $pq = r$ and $q = \dfrac{s}{p}$.

$r = p * \dfrac{s}{p} = s$

62. (B) Known: $\dfrac{a}{b} = 6$.

$\dfrac{2a}{3b} = \dfrac{2}{3}\left(\dfrac{a}{b}\right) = \dfrac{2}{3}(6) = 4$

63. (Grid-in answer = 56)

$$\frac{7\sqrt{x}}{4} = 7\left(\frac{\sqrt{x}}{4}\right) = 7(8) = 56$$

64. (Grid-in answer = 2)

$x = \frac{1}{8}y$ and both x and $y > 1$

The smallest possible values are $x = 2$ and $y = 16$.

65. (D) $\dfrac{x+1}{y} + 8 = \dfrac{x+1}{y} + \dfrac{8y}{y} = \dfrac{x+8y+1}{y}$

66. (A) $-2 < x + 5 < 9$

$-7 < x < 4$

The only solution that can be written in the form $3a$ where a is a positive integer is $x = 3$, because $-7 < 3(1) < 4$.

67. (C) The product of consecutive odd integers m and n where $m < n$,

$m * (m+2) = m^2 + 2m$

68. (C) Known: $a = b + 10$ and $b = c - 7$.

$a = (c-7) + 10 = c + 3$

69. (Grid-in answer = 11)

Known: $x - 4y = 15$ and $2x + 6y = 16$.

Solve for x in terms of y: $2x = 16 - 6y$ $\therefore x = \dfrac{16 - 6y}{2} = 8 - 3y$

Solve for y: $(8 - 3y) - 4y = 15 = 8 - 7y$

$-7y = 15 - 8 = 7$ $\therefore y = -1$

Solve for x using y:

$x - 4(-1) = 15$

$x = 15 - 4 = 11$

70. $\left(\text{Grid-in answer} = \dfrac{1}{2}\right)$

$x^2 = \dfrac{1}{2} * x$

$\dfrac{x^2}{x} = x = \dfrac{1}{2}$

71. **(C)** $8 * 20.5 < 50(x)$

$164 < 50x$

$\dfrac{164}{50} = 3.28 < x$ ∴ You must buy at least four bags.

72. **(B)** Known: $\sqrt{m+n} = 4m$.

$$\left(\sqrt{m+n}\right)^2 = (4m)^2$$

$$m + n = 16m^2$$

73. **(A)** Total pieces $= c$

Pieces used $= 5$

Pieces left $= c - 5$

74. **(A)** $2xy = 26$ for $0 < x < 4$

$xy = 13$

If x is less than 4, y can't be 3 because then $x * y < 13$.

75. (Grid-in answer $= 4$)

$-9x \leq -28$

$\dfrac{-9x}{-9} \geq \dfrac{-28}{-9}$ (when you divide by a negative, flip the inequality sign)

$x \geq \dfrac{28}{9} = 3.1$

$x \geq 3.1$ ∴ the smallest possible integer value of x is 4

76. (Grid-in answer $= 28$)

$\dfrac{1}{4} = \dfrac{3}{a} + \dfrac{1}{7}$

$\dfrac{1}{4} - \dfrac{1}{7} = \dfrac{3}{a}$

$\dfrac{7}{4*7} - \dfrac{4}{7*4} = \dfrac{3}{a}$ (common denominator)

$\dfrac{3}{28} = \dfrac{3}{a}$ ∴ $a = 28$

77. (Grid-in answer $= 26$)

Known: $m = 2n$ and $n = 8 + 5$.

$n = 13$

$m = 2 * 13 = 26$

78. (C) Known: $\dfrac{1}{2}x = \dfrac{1}{4}y$.

Solve for x in terms of y: $x = \dfrac{1}{4}y * \dfrac{2}{1}$ $\therefore x = \dfrac{1}{2}y$

Substitute x in equation $\dfrac{3}{4}x + 1$: $\dfrac{3}{4}\left(\dfrac{1}{2}y\right) + 1$

$\dfrac{3}{8}y + 1$

79. (C) Known: $m\Theta n = 3(m)^2 - n$ and $2\Theta n = 9$.

$2\Theta n = 3(2)^2 - n = 12 - n = 9$

$-n = 9 - 12 = -3 \; \therefore n = 3$

80. (B) Known: $x - 2y = 8$.

Solve for x in terms of y: $x = 8 + 2y$

Substitute into $\dfrac{x}{2} - y$: $\dfrac{8 + 2y}{2} - y = 4 + y - y = 4$

81. (D) $(6\alpha + 5) - (6\alpha - 3) = (6\alpha + 5) - 6\alpha + 3 = 8$

82. (D) $3 < 2x + 1 < 10 \Rightarrow 2 < 2x < 9 \Rightarrow 1 < x < \dfrac{9}{2}$

I. $1 < \dfrac{x}{2} < \dfrac{9}{2} \Rightarrow 2 < x < 9 \Rightarrow$ This overlaps the inequality above and is a possiblity.

II. $1 < 2x < \dfrac{9}{2} \Rightarrow \dfrac{1}{2} < x < \dfrac{9}{4} \Rightarrow$ This overlaps the inequality above and is a possiblity.

III. $1 < 5x < \dfrac{9}{2} \Rightarrow \dfrac{1}{5} < x < \dfrac{9}{10} \Rightarrow$ This does *not* overlap the inequality above.

83. (C) The number of green (g) marbles is 6 more than red (r): $g = r + 6$

Total marbles $= r + g = r + (r + 6) = 2r + 6$

84. $\left(\text{Grid-in answer} = \dfrac{4}{3}\right)$

$x - 2 = 4x - 6$

$-2 = 3x - 6$

$4 = 3x \therefore x = \dfrac{4}{3}$

85. (B) Known: $4p + q = k$ and $p = 2q$.

Substitute for p: $4(2q) + q = 8q + q = k$

$\therefore k = 9q$

86. **(D)** $\dfrac{1}{2}\left(\dfrac{3x}{y}+\dfrac{1}{6}\right)=\dfrac{1}{2}\left(\dfrac{3x*6}{y*6}+\dfrac{1*y}{6*y}\right)=\dfrac{1}{2}\left(\dfrac{18x}{6y}+\dfrac{y}{6y}\right)=\dfrac{1}{2}\left(\dfrac{18x+y}{6y}\right)=\dfrac{18x+y}{12y}$

87. **(D)** $\dfrac{5}{36}=\dfrac{x}{45}$ (Let x be the amount of miles she can run in 45 minutes.)

$x=\dfrac{5}{36}*45=\dfrac{225}{36}=\dfrac{25(9)}{4(9)}=\dfrac{25}{4}$

88. (Grid-in answer $= 14$)

Known: $2ab-a=5$.
Simplify equation: $4ab-2a+4=(4ab-2a)+4=2(2ab-a)+4$
Substitute: $2(2ab-a)+4=2(5)+4=14$

89. **(B)** $3x<\dfrac{11}{2}$ and $-2<x+1<4$

$x<\dfrac{11}{2*3}$ and $-3<x<3$ $\left(\text{Knowing that }\dfrac{11}{6}<3,\ \dfrac{11}{6}\text{ becomes the top bound}\right)$

$-3<x<\dfrac{11}{6}$ There is only one positive integer in that range and it is 1.

90. **(C)** The inequality is only true if m and n have different signs.

91. $\left(\text{Grid-in answer }=\dfrac{17}{16}\right)$

$\sqrt{x-1}=\dfrac{1}{4}\Rightarrow\left(\sqrt{x-1}\right)^2=\left(\dfrac{1}{4}\right)^2\Rightarrow x-1=\dfrac{1}{16}$

$\therefore x=\dfrac{1}{16}+1=\dfrac{1}{16}+\dfrac{16}{16}=\dfrac{17}{16}$

92. **(A)** Known: $a=4b$ and $a>14$.
Substitute $4b$ in for a: $4b>14$
$\therefore b>\dfrac{14}{4}\Rightarrow b>\dfrac{7}{2}$

93. **(D)** Known: $3m-n=10$ and $-2m+4n=8$.

Solve for n: $-2m+4n=8\Rightarrow 4n=8+2m\Rightarrow n=\dfrac{8}{4}+\dfrac{2m}{4}=2+0.5m$
Substitute: $3m-n=10\Rightarrow 3m-(2+0.5m)=10$
$2.5m-2=10\Rightarrow 2.5m=12\ \therefore m=4.8$
Plug back in: $3m-n=10\Rightarrow 3(4.8)-n=10\Rightarrow 14.4-n=10\therefore n=4.4$
$m+3n=4.8+3*(4.4)=18$

94. (D) Known: $\dfrac{2}{3}x = 5y$.

$$y = \frac{2x}{3*5} = \frac{2x}{15}$$

$$\therefore 15y = 15 * \frac{2x}{15} = 2x$$

95. (C) $\dfrac{x \text{ envelopes}}{1 \text{ show}} * \dfrac{y \text{ shows}}{1 \text{ week}} = x * y \dfrac{\text{envelopes}}{\text{week}}$

96. (C) Slope: The slopes of perpendicular lines are negative reciprocals of each other.

$$-\frac{2}{3} \Rightarrow \frac{-1}{\left(-\dfrac{2}{3}\right)} = \frac{3}{2}$$

$m = \dfrac{3}{2}$ and the y-intercept is $b = \dfrac{1}{8}$ because this is where it crosses the axis.

Thus, the equation of the line, $y = mx + b$, is $y = \dfrac{3}{2}x + \dfrac{1}{8}$.

97. (C) If R is the midpoint of $\overline{PQ}$, the length of $\overline{PR}$ is $\dfrac{6}{2} = 3$.

The line $\overline{PS}$ is the same length as $\overline{PR} + \overline{RS} = 3 + 6 = 9$.

98. (A) Slope of $\overline{PQ}$: $\dfrac{y_2 - y_1}{x_2 - x_1} = \dfrac{0 - 0}{5 - (-4)} = 0$

I. Slope of $\overline{QN} = \dfrac{0 - 0}{4 - 5} = 0$ (Parallel to PQ, because it has the same slope)

II. Slope of $\overline{MN} = \dfrac{0 - (-5)}{0 - 4} \neq 0$

III. Slope of $\overline{PM} = \dfrac{-5 - 0}{0 - (-4)} \neq 0$

99. (A) The midpoint formula is

$$\left(\frac{(x_1 + x_2)}{2}, \frac{(y_1 + y_2)}{2}\right) = \left(\frac{(4 + -2)}{2}, \frac{(6 + 6)}{2}\right) = (1, 6)$$

100. (B) Since line ℓ is undefined, it is a vertical line along the y-axis ($x = 0$). That means line m is also a vertical line ($x = 2$). These line are 2 units apart.

101. **(A)** Find slope: The slopes of perpendicular lines are negative reciprocals of each other.

$$3y + x = 4 \Rightarrow 3y = 4 - x \Rightarrow y = \frac{4}{3} - \frac{1}{3}x \text{ (line perpendicular to line } l)$$

$$-\frac{1}{3} \Rightarrow \frac{-1}{\left(-\frac{1}{3}\right)} = \frac{3}{1} = 3$$

y-intercept is -5 because this is where it crosses the y-axis.
Equation: $y = 3y - 5$
Substitute $(-4, t)$: $t = 3(-4) - 5 \Rightarrow t = -17$

102. **(D)** The height of the right triangle is 3 and the base is 1. Using the Pythagorean Theorem, the length of the hypotenuse is $c = \sqrt{a^2 + b^2} = \sqrt{3^2 + 1^2} = \sqrt{10}$.

103. $\left(\text{Grid-in answer} = \dfrac{7}{16}\right)$

The slopes of parallel lines are equal: $p = q$.

$$p + q = \frac{7}{8} \Rightarrow p + p = \frac{7}{8} \Rightarrow 2p = \frac{7}{8} \Rightarrow p = \frac{7}{8*2} = \frac{7}{16}$$

104. **(A)** The total angle between line l and m is 90 degrees because they are parallel.

$$2x + y = 90 \ (2x = y)$$
$$y + y = 90 \Rightarrow 2y = 90 \Rightarrow y = 45$$

105. **(B)** The slopes of parallel lines are equal: $m = n$.

$$mn = c \Rightarrow m^2 = c \Rightarrow m = \sqrt{c}$$

106. **(B)** p and q have the same relationship as w and z because lines m and n are parallel.

$$\therefore w = 2z \Rightarrow z = \frac{w}{2}$$

107. **(D)** The point $(1, 4)$ is 1 unit away from the y-axis and 4 units away from the x-axis.

$$n = 1 \text{ and } m = 4$$
$$m + n = 4 + 1 = 5$$

108. **(B)** Slope-intercept form is $y = mx + b \Rightarrow m = 1 \Rightarrow y = (1)x + b$
Plug in point $(1, 5)$ to find y-intercept: $5 = 1 + b \Rightarrow b = 4$
Equation: $y = x + 4$
(A) $-6 = -10 + 4$
(B) $-3 \neq -8 + 4$ (Does not fall on line.)
(C) $2 = -2 + 4$
(D) $6 = 2 + 4$

109. **(D)** The x-axis has a slope of 0 and parallel lines have equal slopes, so line m has a slope of 0.

Slope of 0 means no change in y, so if it crosses $(5, 2)$, the y value will always be 2.

110. (Grid-in answer = 18)

If B is the midpoint of $\overline{AC}$, and $\overline{BC}$ is 4, then $\overline{AB}$ is also 4.
The total length of the line is $\overline{AB} + \overline{BC} + \overline{CD} = 4 + 4 + 10 = 18$.

111. **(D)** $m + n = 0 \Rightarrow n = -m$

The line with slope $-m$ is parallel to the line with slope n because $n = -m$.

112. **(B)** $x = -5y + 10$
$$x - 10 = -5y$$
$$\frac{-x}{5} + 2 = y$$

In slope-intercept form $y = mx + b \Rightarrow$ slope is $m = -\frac{1}{5}$.

113. **(B)** Slope $= \dfrac{\text{rise}}{\text{run}} = \dfrac{\Delta y}{\Delta x} = \dfrac{1 - (-1)}{2 - 6} = -\dfrac{2}{4} = -\dfrac{1}{2}$

Plug in point $(2, 1)$ into $y = \dfrac{-x}{2} + b$ to find b: $1 = -\dfrac{2}{2} + b \Rightarrow b = 2$.

Equation: $y = \dfrac{-x}{2} + 2$

At $y = 3$: $3 = \dfrac{-a}{2} + 2 \Rightarrow 1 = \dfrac{-a}{2} \Rightarrow 2 = -a \therefore a = -2$

114. **(D)** Plug in $(0, 0)$ to each equation and see which expression is true.
(a) $0 + 5(0) = -2$: *False*
(b) $-3(0) - (0) = 1$: *False*
(c) $2(0) + 2(0) = -1$: *False*
(d) $3(0) - 4(0) = 0$: *True*

115. **(C)** Original cordinates of point D $(2, 3)$

Reflect over x-axis by changing the sign of the y-coordinate. $\Rightarrow (2, -3)$

116. **(B)** Find the slope between each pair of points using $m = \dfrac{\Delta y}{\Delta x}$.

(A) $m = \dfrac{5 - 0}{0 - (-5)} = 1$

(B) $m = \dfrac{0 - 5}{5 - (0)} = -1$ (This is the answer.)

(C) $m = 1$

(D) $m = $ undefined

117. **(B)** With an hour pause after 3 hours of driving, the family will take 3 breaks
on their 12-hour trip. $\dfrac{12}{(3+1)} = 3$ breaks. During a break the slope is zero. Graph B
is the only graph with three breaks.

118. **(A)** An undefined slope is a vertical line and Δx is 0.

   All points on line m will have x-coordinate -7, so A is the only point that can be
   on the line.

119. **(D)** The distance between the center and a point on its circumference is the radius.

   Use distance formula to find radius: $\sqrt{(4-1)^2 + (6-3)^2} = \sqrt{3^2 + 3^2} = \sqrt{18}$.

   The area of a circle is $A = \pi * r^2$: $A = \pi * \left(\sqrt{18}\right)^2 = 18\pi$.

120. **(B)** The area of a circle is πr^2, which is equal to 9π. Thus, $\pi R^2 = 9\pi \Rightarrow R^2 = 9 \Rightarrow R = 3$.
Plugging this into the circumference formula: $2\pi R = 2\pi(3) = 6\pi$

121. **(C)** A point on the y-axis has an x-coordinate of zero.

   $\therefore$ no matter where point P is, the product of the x-coordinates of P and Q is 0.

122. **(D)** The plane flies a total of 3 hours north and 3 hours west.

   Going 200 mph, the plane will move 600 miles in 3 hours. ($3 * 200 = 600$)
   North is in the positive Y direction, and west is in the negative X direction,
   so it will end at $(-600, 600)$.

123. **(D)** Known: $a - c = 5$ and $b - d = 15$ and slope $= \dfrac{\Delta y}{\Delta x} = \dfrac{(y_2 - y_1)}{x_2 - x_1}$.

   With points (a, b) and (c, d): slope $= \dfrac{b-d}{a-c} = \dfrac{15}{5} = 3$.

124. **(D)** D is the midpoint of $\overline{CE}$, so because $\overline{CD}$ is length 3, so is $\overline{DE}$.

   Adding the known lengths: $\overline{AB} + \overline{CD} + \overline{DE} = 3 + 3 + 3 = 9$. (This leaves out the
   unknown $\overline{BC}$.)
   $\therefore$ The length of $\overline{AE} \geq 9$ (Only answer D fits this inequality.)

125. **(A)** PQ has a slope of $m = \dfrac{\Delta y}{\Delta x}$. From point R to point P, the Δx is the same,

   but the Δy is $\dfrac{1}{2}$ that from Q to P. $\therefore$ slope of $\overline{PR} = \dfrac{(1/2)\Delta y}{\Delta x} = \dfrac{1}{2}\left(\dfrac{\Delta y}{\Delta x}\right) = \dfrac{1}{2}m$

126. **(C)** Parallel lines never intersect, cannot share points, and have the same slope.

Find the slope of the first line: $m = \dfrac{\Delta y}{\Delta x} = \dfrac{5-4}{0-(-1)} = \dfrac{1}{1} = 1$

Equation of first line : $y = (1)x + 5$

y-intercept is $(0, 5)$

See which of the answers do not lie on the first line by plugging the point coordinate values into the equation.

(A) $-5 = (-10) + 5$: *True*

(B) $0 = (-5) + 5$: *True*

(C) $6 = (-2) + 5$: *False* (Does not lie on first line $\therefore$ could be on the other line)

(D) $8 = (3) + 5$: *True*

127. **(A)** When reflecting over $y = x$, simply switch the x- and the y-coordinates.

Point $P(3, 9) \Rightarrow (9,3)$

128. (Grid-in answer $= 9$)

$$\frac{\pi(3R)^2}{\pi R^2} = \frac{9R^2}{R^2} = 9$$

129. **(A)** Plug $(-2, -1)$ into $y = 2x + b$ to find the y-intercept.

$-1 = 2(-2) + b \Rightarrow b = 3 \Rightarrow$ Line n must cross the y-axis at $(0, 3)$.

$\therefore$ Choice (A) cannot be on the line because it is not the y-intercept.

130. **(A)** Circle B has a circumference of $2\pi(3R)$. Circle A has a diameter of $2R$. The ratio of B's circumference to A's diameter is: $\dfrac{2\pi(3R)}{2R} = 3\pi$.

131. **(B)** Find slope of perpendicular: $m = \dfrac{\Delta y}{\Delta x} = \dfrac{6-2}{(-2)-8} = \dfrac{4}{-10}$

Perpendicular lines have negative reciprocal slopes: $-\dfrac{1}{m} = \dfrac{10}{4} = \dfrac{5}{2}$

Find the answer with a matching slope by putting them in point-slope form.

(A) $y = \dfrac{-2x + 20}{5}$

(B) $y = \dfrac{5x - 12}{2}$ (Slope matches.)

(C) $y = \dfrac{-5x + 14}{2}$

(D) $y = \dfrac{2x - 15}{5}$

132. (C) Costs of x dozen cupcakes: $3.25x$

Earnings from selling x dozen cupcakes: $1.50 * (12) * x = 18x$

Net profit $= 18x - 3.25x$

133. (C) $\dfrac{-3}{8} \le \dfrac{m}{-2} + 8 \le 7 \Rightarrow \dfrac{-3}{8} - 8 \le \dfrac{m}{-2} \le 7 - 8 \Rightarrow \dfrac{-3}{8} - \dfrac{64}{8} \le \dfrac{m}{-2} \le -1$

$\dfrac{-67}{8} \le \dfrac{m}{-2} \le -1 \Rightarrow \dfrac{-67}{8}(-2) \ge m \ge (-1)(-2)$

(Flip inequality signs when dividing by a negative on both sides.)

$\dfrac{67}{4} \ge m \ge 2$. $m = 2$ is the only option that fits into this range.

134. (A) Find y: $y - 8 = 24 \Rightarrow y = 32$

Find x by substituting y: $\dfrac{x}{2} = 2 + \dfrac{1}{2}y = 2 + \dfrac{32}{2} = 18 \Rightarrow x = 18 * 2 = 36$

$x^2 - y^2 = (36)^2 - (32)^2 = 272$

135. $\left(\text{Grid-in answer} = \dfrac{1}{11} \right)$

$\dfrac{2}{x} - 10 = 12 \Rightarrow \dfrac{2}{x} = 12 + 10$

$\dfrac{2}{x} = 22 \Rightarrow 2 = 22x \Rightarrow x = \dfrac{2}{22} = \dfrac{1}{11}$

136. (B) $3x = 8y - 3 \Rightarrow x = \dfrac{8y - 3}{3}$

Substitution: $4y + 2x = 5 \Rightarrow 4y + 2\left(\dfrac{8y-3}{3}\right) = 5 \Rightarrow 4y + 2\left(\dfrac{8}{3}y - \dfrac{3}{3}\right) = 5$

$4y + 2\left(\dfrac{8}{3}y - 1\right) = 5 \Rightarrow 4y + \dfrac{16y}{3} - 2 = 5 \Rightarrow \dfrac{12y + 16y}{3} = 7$

$\Rightarrow 28y = 21 \Rightarrow y = \dfrac{21}{28} = \dfrac{3}{4}$

Find x: $x = \dfrac{8y - 3}{3} = \dfrac{8(0.75) - 3}{3} = \dfrac{6 - 3}{3} = 1$

Solve: $\dfrac{x}{y} = \dfrac{1}{(3/4)} = \dfrac{4}{3}$

137. (A) Amount of gallons: $\dfrac{150 \text{ miles}}{x \text{ miles per gallon}}$

Total cost: $\$4 * \left(\dfrac{150}{x}\right)$

Cost per person: $\dfrac{\$4 * \left(\dfrac{150}{x}\right)}{2} = 2 * \dfrac{150}{x}$

138. (C) $x + 4y = 6 \Rightarrow x = 6 - 4y$
$2x - 1 = 4(y + 2) \Rightarrow 2(6 - 4y) - 1 = 4y + 8 \Rightarrow 12 - 8y - 1 = 4y + 8$
$11 - 8y = 4y + 8 \Rightarrow 11 - 8 = 12y \Rightarrow y = \dfrac{3}{12} = \dfrac{1}{4}$
$x = 6 - 4y = 6 - 4\left(\dfrac{1}{4}\right) = 5$
$x + y = 5 + \dfrac{1}{4} = \dfrac{20}{4} + \dfrac{1}{4} = \dfrac{21}{4}$

139. (B) $2y + 5x = -11 \Rightarrow y = \dfrac{-5x - 11}{2} \therefore m = \dfrac{-5}{2}$

To be perpendicular, slopes must be negative reciprocals of each other.
Put the answers in point-slope form, and see which one does not have a
slope of $-\dfrac{1}{m} = \dfrac{2}{5}$.
(A) $y = \dfrac{2}{5}x + \dfrac{3}{10}$
(B) $y = \dfrac{5}{2}x + 6$ (only line with the wrong slope $\therefore$ Answer)
(C) $y = \dfrac{2}{5}x + \dfrac{1}{2}$
(D) $y = \dfrac{-2}{-5}x + \dfrac{-4}{-5}$

140. (A) $-59 \geq -3x - 5 \geq -110$
$-54 \geq -3x \geq -105$
$\dfrac{-54}{-3} \leq x \leq \dfrac{-105}{-3}$ (Flip the inequality signs when dividing by a negative.)
$18 \leq x \leq 35$

141. (D) Solve for $3a$ in terms of b: $3a + 2b = 33 \Rightarrow 3a = 33 - 2b$
Substitution: $a - 5b = -2a - 9 \Rightarrow 3a - 5b = -9 \Rightarrow 33 - 2b - 5b = -9$
$33 - 7b = -9 \Rightarrow -7b = -9 - 33 \Rightarrow b = \dfrac{42}{7} = 6$
$3a = 33 - 2b = 33 - 2(6) = 21 \Rightarrow a = 7$
$a + b = 7 + 6 = 13$

142. (D) $a_n = 1 - a_{n-1}$ and $a_1 = 2$
$a_2 = 1 - a_{2-1} = 1 - 2 = -1,$
$a_3 = 1 - a_{3-1} = 1 - (-1) = 2$

143. (C) In 2000 they spent 5 ($25,000) and in 2010 they spent 3 ($25,000).
$(5 - 3)(25,000) = 2 * 25,000 = \$50,000$

144. (Grid-in answer = 6.37)

Round 3.174 to the nearest tenth: 3.2
Round 3.174 to the nearest hundredth: 3.17
$3.2 + 3.17 = 6.37$

145. (Grid-in answer = −2)

$a_n = (m) * a_{n-1}$
$a_3 = m * a_2$ and $a_2 = m * a_1$ and $a = 4$
$\therefore a_3 = m * m * 4 = 16 \Rightarrow m = \pm \sqrt{\dfrac{16}{4}} = \pm 2$
The only way the sixth term could be negative is if m is negative $\therefore m = -2$

146. (**D**) Known: $m \Pi n = 2m - 4n$.

$3\Pi(-2) = 2(3) - 4(-2) = 6 + 8 = 14$

147. (**B**) A prime number is a number that is greater than 1 and only has 1 and itself as factors.

The smallest prime number is 2, so $a = 2$.
$4a = 2b^{\frac{1}{2}} \Rightarrow 4(2) = 2b^{\frac{1}{2}} \Rightarrow \dfrac{4(2)}{2} = b^{\frac{1}{2}}$
$b^{\frac{1}{2}} = \sqrt{b} = 4 \Rightarrow b = 4^2 = 16$

148. (**D**) Known: $8 < h < 14$.

$8 - 11 < h - 11 < 14 - 11$
$-3 < (h - 11) < 3 \Rightarrow |h - 11| < 3$

149. (**B**) Known: $x(\therefore)y = 3xy$ and $\partial x = 5x - 1$.

$\partial x = 5x - 1 = 14 \Rightarrow 5x = 15 \Rightarrow x = \dfrac{15}{5} = 3$
$5x(\therefore)2 = 3(5x)(2) = 2y \Rightarrow 3(5 * 3) *2 = 2y \Rightarrow 45 * 2 = 2y \Rightarrow y = 4$
$3y = 3(45) = 135$

150. (**C**) $|4x - 9| = 19$

$(4x - 9) = 19$ or $(4x - 9) = -19$
$4x = 28$ or $4x = -10$
$x = 7$ or $\dfrac{-10}{4}$ (if $x > 0$, x must equal 7)

151. (Grid-in answer = 84)

Possible values: 42, 84. Both are divisible by 6 and 14, but the problem specifies the larger value.

152. (C) $\sqrt{n} > 5 \Rightarrow n > 5^2$

$\sqrt[m]{n} > \sqrt[m]{5^2}$

Because $\sqrt[m]{5^2} > \sqrt[m]{5}$, $\sqrt[m]{n}$ must be larger than $\sqrt[m]{5}$.

153. (D) $a_n = \dfrac{a_{n-1}}{2} \Rightarrow a_n * 2 = a_{n-1}$

$a_4 = a_5 * 2 = 10 * 2 = 20 \Rightarrow a_3 = a_4 * 2 = 40$

$a_2 = a_3 * 2 = 80 \Rightarrow a_1 = a_2 * 2 = 160$

154. (D) $x - 5 > 7$

$x > 12$

155. (D) $(xy)^2 = 36 \Rightarrow xy = \sqrt{36} = \pm 6$

$x * y = \pm 6$ (factors of 6 are: 1, 2, 3, 6)
(A) $-5 = -3 - 2$
(B) $-1 = 3 - 2$
(C) $5 = 6 - 1$
(D) $\dfrac{25}{2}$ The answer because for any two positive whole numbers the sum $\leq$ the product.

156. (C) Find the ratio of the geometric sequence by $\dfrac{a_{n+1}}{a_n}$.

Ratio $= \dfrac{-4}{16} = -\dfrac{1}{4}$

Find : $a_5 = a_4 *$ ratio $= \dfrac{-1}{4} * \dfrac{-1}{4} = \dfrac{1}{16}$

157. (D) $A(7) = t^2 + 2t = (7)^2 + 2(7) = 49 + 14 = 63$

$B(7) = 10t = 10(7) = 70$

158. (B) $b = \dfrac{3}{|-a|} = \dfrac{3}{a} \Rightarrow$ Solving for a: $a = \dfrac{3}{b}$. Now plug in each possible value for b:

(A) $a = \dfrac{3}{-3/16} = -16$ (*not* a positive integer)

(B) $a = \dfrac{3}{3/5} = 5$ (positive integer)

(C) $a = \dfrac{3}{2}$ (*not* an integer)

(D) $a = \dfrac{3}{11}$ (*not* an integer)

159. (C) $2x+4=4(x-2) \Rightarrow 2x+4=4x-8 \Rightarrow 4+8=2x \Rightarrow x=6$
$-x+k=2x-1 \Rightarrow -6+k=2(6)-1 \Rightarrow k=11+6 \Rightarrow k=17$

160. (C) Neither a nor b can be 0 because that would cause $a=d$ or $b=d$.
Since a and b are nonzero, and $a*b*c=0 \Rightarrow c=0$.

161. (C)

(A) $a^2+b^2 \Rightarrow$ The sum of the square of 2 even numbers must be *even*.

(B) $(a+1)^2+(b+1)^2 \Rightarrow$ The sum of the squares of two odd numbers must be *even*.

(C) $(a+1)*(b+1)^2 \Rightarrow$ The product of two odd numbers must be *odd*.

(D) $a+b \Rightarrow$ The sum of two even numbers must be *even*.

162. (A)

I. $x^5 < |x| \Rightarrow$ *true* because a negative number raised to an odd power is always negative.

II. $x < \sqrt{(-x)} \Rightarrow$ *true* because the left side is negative and the right side is positive.

III. $\dfrac{x-1}{|x|} < 0 \Rightarrow$ *true* because the numerator is negative and the denominator is positive.

163. (C) Slope of line l : $\dfrac{y_2-y_1}{x_2-x_1} = \dfrac{a-0}{0-(-2)} = \dfrac{a}{2}$
Slope of line j : $\dfrac{y_2-y_1}{x_2-x_1} = \dfrac{2-0}{6-(4)} = \dfrac{2}{2}$
Slopes of parallel lines are equal: $\dfrac{2}{2} = \dfrac{a}{2} \therefore a=2$

164. (B)

I. $a^2 < b^2 < c^2 \Rightarrow$ *false* because $a^2 > 0$ and a^2 may be a large number greater than b^2 and c^2.

II. $c-b > a \Rightarrow$ Always *true* since $a < 0$ and $c > b$.

III. $c+a > b \Rightarrow$ *false* if a is large and negative.

165. (B) Since $m^2 < m$, then $0 < m < 1$. Also, it's given that $n > 0$.

(A) $mn < 0 \Rightarrow$ *false* because both m and n are positive

(B) $\dfrac{n}{m} > n \Rightarrow n > mn \Rightarrow 1 > m \Rightarrow$ *true*

(C) $mn > n \Rightarrow m > 1 \Rightarrow$ *false*

(D) $n^2 > m^2 \Rightarrow$ may be *false* if $m=n$

Section 2

166. (B) Total number of possible outcomes (integers $1 < x < 15$): 13

Total number of desired outcomes (integers $1 < x < 5$): 3

Probability $= \dfrac{3}{13}$

167. (Grid-in answer $= 32$)

Mean = Sum of total terms divided by number of different terms

$4 = \dfrac{\text{Sum of terms}}{8} \Rightarrow \text{Sum} = 4 * 8 = 32$

168. (C) Set number of blue coins as B and red coins as R.

$R = 2B$ and Total $= R + B$

Probability $= \dfrac{\text{Desired}}{\text{Total}} = \dfrac{B}{R+B} = \dfrac{B}{(2B)+B} = \dfrac{B}{3B} = \dfrac{1}{3}$

169. (D) Larger circle area $= \pi r^2$

Smaller circle area $= (0.5)\pi r^2$ (because it is half of the bigger)

Average $= \dfrac{\text{Total sum}}{\text{Total number}} = \dfrac{(\pi r^2) + \left(\dfrac{1}{2}\right)\pi r^2}{2} = \dfrac{\dfrac{3}{2}\pi r^2}{2} = \dfrac{3\pi r^2}{4}$

170. (C) The median (middle value) of the first list is $n_3 = 3$. If 5 is added to every number in the list, the median will shift up by 5 too.

Median $= 3 + 5 = 8$

171. (Grid-in answer $= 17$)

In a case where the median falls between two numbers on the list, the average is the median.

The median of the list of 10 is between the fifth and the sixth.

Therefore, the mean of the fifth and sixth number is the median (14).

Mean $= \dfrac{\text{Total sum}}{\text{Total number}} \Rightarrow 14 = \dfrac{11 + n_6}{2}$

$14 * 2 = 11 + n_6 \Rightarrow 28 - 11 = n_6 \Rightarrow n_6 = 17$

172. (C) There are 11 people in front of her and behind her. (Don't forget to count Jackie!)

$11 + 1 + 11 = 23$

173. (Grid-in answer = 4)

Count the total number of patrons: $25 + 15 + 35 + 10 + 5 + 2 = 92$
There are 92 people in the list, so the mean number of plays attended by the 46th and 47th patron is the median. If you count from the front or back, the 46th and 47th patron will fall in the range of 4 plays attended. ∴ median = 4.

174. **(C)** Because Matt is sleeping for 9 hours and one day lasts 24 hours, then the probability will be $\dfrac{9}{24} = \dfrac{3}{8}$.

175. $\left(\text{Grid-in answer} = \dfrac{1}{2} \right)$

Half the integers from 1 to 10 are odd and half are even, so there is a 1 in 2 chance the player will earn 2 points.

176. **(B)** Total number of possible outcomes: $7 + 2 + 1 = 10$

Total number of desired outcomes: $10 - 7 = 3$

Probability $= \dfrac{3}{10}$

177. **(C)** From 1 to 20, the multiples of 3 or 7 are 3, 6, 7, 9, 12, 14, 15, and 18. This means that there are 8 possible desired outcomes out of 20, or $\dfrac{8}{20}$, which when rationalized (reduced by 4) is equal to answer choice (C).

178. **(B)** There are 4 jacks, 4 queens, and 4 kings, meaning that the total probabilities possible are $3 * 4 = 12$. Then, the probability can be calculated by $\dfrac{12}{52}$, which is equal to answer choice (B) when rationalized.

179. **(A)** May has one-half of a symbol more than January.

Half a symbol is worth $\dfrac{500}{2} = 250$.

180. **(C)** There are nine different ways the first officer can be selected:

eight for the second and seven for the third (because you cannot pick someone twice). $9 * 8 * 7 = 504$ different ways

181. (Grid-in answer = 1)

A median only depends on the center value of the list of five when ordered smallest to largest.
The numbers before the median can be any number lower. The smallest positive integer is 1.

182. **(A)** To find the number of ways in this case you multiply the number of options of each, because you are finding the possible combinations and order does not matter.

183. **(B)** There are 20 possible ways to pick the first, and after that 19 ways to pick the second.
∴ the number of ways ushers can be selected $= 20 * 19 = 380$.

184. $\left(\text{Grid-in answer} = \dfrac{1}{6}\right)$

There are six sides to the die. The probability of getting any one side is $\dfrac{1}{6}$.

185. **(D)** There are six possibilities when picking the first and still six ways to pick the second.
∴ the number of ways $= 6 * 6 = 36$.

186. **(C)** The correct answer is 6 because the point farthest from the line of best fit, which shows a general positive increase, is point $(6, 7)$.

187. **(C)** The list goes: 15, 25, 35, 45, 55, 65, 75, 85.
The median falls between 45 and 55 and is the average.
$\dfrac{45 + 55}{2} = 50$

188. **(A)** Convert 15 minutes to hours: $15 * \left(\dfrac{1 \text{ hour}}{60 \text{ min}}\right) = \dfrac{15}{60} = \dfrac{1}{4}$

Distance = Speed times Time $= m(\text{mph}) * \dfrac{1}{4}(\text{hours}) = \dfrac{m}{4}$ miles

189. **(D)** The length of B is five times that of A, and they are similar, so the width of B is 5 times A.
The width of $A = w$, so $5w$ is the width of B.

190. **(C)** $y = m * x$ (because they are directly related)
$m = \dfrac{y}{x} = \dfrac{c^3}{c^2} = c$
$\therefore y = cx = 5c$

191. (C) This can be calculated by transforming A, B, C, and D into the corresponding $4x$, $3x$, $7x$, and $2x$. Then, we know that

$A = 60 + D$

$4x = 60 + 2x$

$2x = 30$

$x = 15$

Then, the total number of B letters is $3x$, which means that $3 * 15 = 45$.

192. (C) In an inverse relationship, $m = c\dfrac{1}{n}$

Plugging in $m = 5$ and $n = 1 \Rightarrow 5 = c\dfrac{1}{1} \Rightarrow c = 5$

Thus, $m = \dfrac{5}{n}$. Plugging in $n = x$, then $m = \dfrac{5}{x}$

193. $\left(\text{Grid-in answer} = \dfrac{15}{8} \right)$

Ratio: $\dfrac{2 \text{ cups of flour}}{3 \text{ cups of sugar}}$

$\dfrac{1\frac{1}{4} \text{ cups of flour}}{x \text{ cups of sugar}} = \dfrac{2}{3} \Rightarrow x = 1\dfrac{1}{4} * \dfrac{3}{2} = \dfrac{5}{4} * \dfrac{3}{2} = \dfrac{15}{8}$

194. (B) The largest increase comes between weeks 2 and 3. This is reflected graphically.

195. (D) Because action and horror together make up 50% and half the pie, comedy and animated categories add up to 50% as well.

196. (C) $a = C * b$ (because they are directly proportional and C is a constant)

$18 = C * 3 \Rightarrow C = 6 \Rightarrow$ Relationship is $A = 6b$

$b = \dfrac{1}{3}$, then $A = 6 * \dfrac{1}{3} = 2$

197. $\left(\text{Grid-in answer} = \dfrac{3}{4} \right)$

$60 \text{ ft} * \dfrac{1}{80} = \dfrac{60}{80} = \dfrac{3}{4} \text{ft}$

198. **(C)** Area of a triangle $= \dfrac{1}{2}$ Length * Height

Height of $A = \dfrac{1}{3}$ Height of B, and A is similar with B, so the length of A will also be one-third that of B.

$$\text{Area}(A) = \frac{1}{2}\text{Length}(A) * \text{Height}(A) = \frac{1}{2} * \frac{\text{Length}(B)}{3} * \frac{\text{Height}(B)}{3}$$

$$\text{Area}(A) = \frac{1}{9}\left(\frac{1}{2}\text{Length}(B) * \text{Height}(B)\right) = \frac{1}{9} * \text{Area}(B)$$

199. **(D)** $\dfrac{x}{y} = \dfrac{2}{7}$

Cross-multiplying yields: $7x = 7y$

200. **(B)** This can be calculated by first considering that $\dfrac{x}{60} = 15\%$, where x is the amount of alcohol in ml.

A transformation yields that $\dfrac{x}{60} = \dfrac{15}{100}$, which is equal to $\dfrac{x}{60} = \dfrac{3}{20}$.

After cross-multiplying and simplifying, we reach $x = 9$.

Then, we need to consider how much water we need to add using the following

$\dfrac{9}{y} = \dfrac{10}{100}$, where y is the total volume of water necessary to have a 10% level of alcohol in the sanitizer. By simplifying this calculation, we get $y = 90$. This means that the total volume of water that needs to be added is 90 ml – 60 ml = 30 ml.

201. (Grid-in answer = 600)

$$80\% = \frac{80}{100}$$

$$\frac{80}{100} * x = 480 \Rightarrow x = 480 * \frac{100}{80} = 600$$

202. **(A)** The points (2, 2) and (5, 5) are the only two that represent a student with the same rank in both sports.

203. $\left(\text{Grid-in answer} = \dfrac{27}{5} \text{ or } 5.4\right)$

Let the one-way distance be d, the time for part 1 of the trip t_1, and the time for part 2 of the trip t_2.

The total trip time $t_1 + t_2 = 45 \text{ min} = \dfrac{45 \text{ min}}{60(\text{min/hour})} = \dfrac{3}{4} \text{hours}$

Solving for $t_1 \Rightarrow t_1 = \dfrac{3}{4} - t_2$.

$d = vt$, so for part 1 of the trip, $d = 12t_1$, and part 2 of the trip, $d = 18t_2$. Because the distance is the same there and back, $12t_1 = 18t_2$.

Plugging in for $t_1 \Rightarrow 12\left(\dfrac{3}{4} - t_2\right) = 18t_2$

Dividing by $12 \Rightarrow \left(\dfrac{3}{4} - t_2\right) = \dfrac{18t_2}{12}$.

Solving for $t_2 \Rightarrow \dfrac{3}{4} = \dfrac{3t_2}{2} + t_2 \Rightarrow \dfrac{3}{4} = \left(\dfrac{3}{2} + 1\right)t_2 \Rightarrow \dfrac{3}{4} = \left(\dfrac{5}{2}\right)t_2 \Rightarrow t_2 = \dfrac{3}{10}$.

$d = 18t_2 = 18\left(\dfrac{3}{10}\right) = \dfrac{27}{5}$

Check: $d = 12t_1 = 12\left(\dfrac{3}{4} - t_2\right) = 12\left(\dfrac{3}{4} - \dfrac{3}{10}\right) = \dfrac{27}{5}$

204. (A) 5 dinner plates (din): 3 dessert plates (des)

$\text{des} = \dfrac{3}{5}\text{din}$ and $\text{din} + \text{des} = n$

$\text{din} + \dfrac{3}{5}\text{din} = n \Rightarrow \dfrac{5}{5}\text{din} + \dfrac{3}{5}\text{din} = n \Rightarrow \dfrac{8}{5}\text{din} = n$

$\therefore \text{din} = \dfrac{5}{8}n$

205. (C) $\text{Percent} = \dfrac{\text{Part}}{\text{Whole}} * 100$

$\dfrac{x}{5x} * 100 = \dfrac{100}{5} = 20\%$

206. (D) $10\% = \dfrac{10}{100} = \dfrac{1}{10} \Rightarrow 10\%$ of $\$m = \dfrac{1}{10}m$

The price of the item is $\left(m - \dfrac{m}{10}\right) = \dfrac{9}{10}m.$

207. (B) $\dfrac{1}{x}\% = \dfrac{\left(\dfrac{1}{x}\right)}{100} = \dfrac{1}{100x} \Rightarrow \dfrac{1}{x}\%$ of $\dfrac{25}{y} = \dfrac{1}{100x} * \dfrac{25}{y} = \dfrac{1}{4xy}$

208. (D) $0.06\% = \dfrac{6}{100}\% = \dfrac{6}{100} * \dfrac{1}{100} = \dfrac{6}{10,000}$

0.06% of x is $6 \Rightarrow \dfrac{6}{10,000} * x = 6 \Rightarrow x = 6 * \dfrac{10,000}{6} = 10,000$

209. (D) 2 machines every 3 days = 1 machine every $1\dfrac{1}{2}$ days.

$\dfrac{20 \text{ days}}{\left(\dfrac{3}{2}\right)(\text{machines per day})} = 20 * \dfrac{2}{3} = \dfrac{40}{3} = 13\dfrac{1}{3} \Rightarrow 13$ complete machines

210. (D) Let x be a number such that $x * 15\% = 35$.

Solve for x: $x * \dfrac{15}{100} = 35 \Rightarrow x = 35 * \dfrac{100}{15} = 7 * \dfrac{100}{3}$

Find 3% of x: $3\%(x) = \dfrac{3}{100} * \left(7 * \dfrac{100}{3}\right) = 7$

211. $\left(\text{Grid-in answer} = \dfrac{5}{2}\right)$

The ratio of x to y is 1:3; therefore $\dfrac{1}{3}y = x$.

Substitute into $y = x + 1$: $y = \dfrac{1}{3}y + 1 \Rightarrow \dfrac{2}{3}y = 1 \Rightarrow y = \dfrac{3}{2}$

The ratio of y to x is 3:5; therefore: $y = \dfrac{3}{5}z$ and $z = \dfrac{5}{3}y \therefore z = \dfrac{5}{3}\left(\dfrac{3}{2}\right) = \dfrac{5}{2}$

212. (B) Sales in July for Jefferson City were approximately 43,000 (±2000), and sales in August for Jefferson City were approximately 37,000 (±2000).

August and July sales add up to about 79,000 (±4000).

213. (A) $\dfrac{\text{Total sum}}{\text{Number of points}} = \dfrac{5x + 3x + 2x + 8x}{4} = \dfrac{18x}{4} = \dfrac{9x}{2}$

214. (A) The events are independent events, so the probability of both occurring is the probability of A times B.

$.25 * 0.30 = 0.075$

215. (Grid-in answer = 20)

First find how many in the group are older than 25 using the probability, and then subtract it from the whole.

$$80 * \frac{3}{4} = 60 \Rightarrow 80 - 60 = 20 \text{ people 25 years old or younger.}$$

216. **(C)** First, put the list in numerical order: 1, 1, 4, 6, 12

See that the number 4 is three places from the left and right of the set, so it is the median.

217. **(D)** Total number of possible passwords: $10^4 = 10,000$

Probability of all the digits being odd: $\left(\frac{5}{10}\right)^4 = \frac{1}{2^4} = \frac{1}{16}$

Total number of passwords with only odd digits: $10,000 * \frac{1}{16} = 625$

218. **(D)** $15 * 14 * 13 * 12 = 32,760$

219. **(C)** Total sum of p, q, and r is $12 * 3 = 36$

Sum of p, q, r, and m is $36 + m$

$$\text{Average} = \frac{\text{Total sum}}{\text{Number of points}} \Rightarrow 20 = \frac{36 + m}{4} \Rightarrow m = 20(4) - 36 = 44$$

220. **(B)** The ratio of seniors to total students is 5:9, so the ratio of seniors to juniors is 5:(9 − 5) or 5:4.

That means if there are 15 seniors (5 * 3), there are 12 juniors (4 * 3).

221. (Grid-in answer = 6)

For the number to be less than 2000, the digit in the thousands place must be 1.

That leaves three numbers {4, 6, 8} to be arranged in the last three spots. $3! = 3 * 2 * 1 = 6$ ways.

222. **(A)** $\dfrac{(2x) + (x + 4) + (5)}{3} = \dfrac{3x + 9}{3} = x + 3$

223. (Grid-in answer = 72)

Let a represent number of appetizers, e represent entrée choices, and d represent dessert. $a = 2e$ and $d = a + 5$. When $a = 4$, $e = (0.5) * a = (0.5) * 4 = 2$ and $d = 4 + 5 = 9$.

Number of possible specials: $a * e * d = 4 * 2 * 9 = 72$ specials.

224. (Grid-in answer = 150)

If the numbers are consecutive, the middle number will be the mean (if the set is odd) and the middle number is always the median. The mean is 150, so therefore the median = 150.

225. **(A)** There are a total of 179 people. The median-aged person will fall 90th in line if you put them in age order. That means he will *have* to fall in the range of the 150 people younger than 38.

226. **(D)** 75% = 0.75 and 100% − 75% = 25% = .25

Average = (0.75) * 82 + (0.25) * 79 = 61.5 + 19.75 = 81.25

227. **(C)** From *A* to *B* there are three path options, and from *B* to *C* there are four path options.

Therefore, total possibilities = 3 * 4 = 12.

228. $\left(\text{Grid-in answer} = \dfrac{1}{18}\right)$

Zero is not a possibility for the first digit of a two-digit number, so there are nine possibilities for the first digit (1–9) and ten for the second (0–9), for a total of 9 * 10 = 90 possible two-digit numbers. Because there are five two-digit numbers less than 15, the probability is $\dfrac{5}{90} = \dfrac{1}{18}$.

229. **(B)** $\dfrac{\text{Total sum}}{\text{Total number}} = \dfrac{(2x^2) + (4x)}{2} = x^2 + 2x$

230. **(B)** Let h_s be the height of the small triangle and h_l be the height of the larger.

$h_l = 3h_s$ and Average $= \dfrac{\text{Sum}}{\text{Number}} = \dfrac{\text{Area}_l + \text{Area}_s}{2} = \dfrac{\frac{1}{2}L*h_l + \frac{1}{2}L*h_s}{2}$

$= \dfrac{L*h_l + L*h_s}{4} = 10$

Solve for the area of the smaller triangle:

$\dfrac{L*(3h_s) + L*(h_s)}{4} = \dfrac{4L*h_s}{4} = L*h_s = 10 \Rightarrow \text{Area} = \dfrac{1}{2}L*h_s = \dfrac{1}{2}(10) = 5$

231. **(C)** There are six possible numbers that could be picked: {4, 6, 7, 14, 18, 21}.

It you subtract 2 from them all, the list becomes {2, 4, 5, 12, 16, 19}.

Three of those are perfectly divisible by 4 and will have remainder 0: {4, 12, 16}.

$\dfrac{3}{6} = \dfrac{1}{2}$

232. (C) Before the teacher brings a new box, there are the same amount of blue and orange boxes.

If after one blue box is added, there are five blue boxes, which means that before there were four blue boxes.

Therefore, there must still be four orange boxes and a total amount of $5 + 4 = 9$, so the probability is $\dfrac{4}{9}$.

233. (A) For x as the median (middle number), use the set $\left\{-2x, x, x^2\right\}$.

(A) If $x = 2$, then the set becomes $\{-4, 2, 4\}$, so x is the median.

(B) If $x = \dfrac{1}{2}$, then the set becomes $\left\{-1, \dfrac{1}{2}, \dfrac{1}{4}\right\}$, so x is *not* the median.

(C) If $x = -1$, then the set becomes $\{2, -1, 1\}$, so x is *not* the median.

(D) If $x = -2$, then the set becomes $\{4, -2, 4\}$, so x is *not* the median.

234. (Grid-in answer = 120)

$5 * 4 * 3 * 2 = 120$

235. (D) If $0 < x < 1$, it will be a fraction and get smaller when you multiply it by itself. Therefore, $3x > x > x^2 > x^3 > x^4$, so x^2 is the median.

236. (A) If angle A is 150 degrees, angle B is $180 - 150 = 30$ degrees.

The chance that a point will be chosen in section B is $\dfrac{30 \text{ degrees}}{360 \text{ degrees}} = \dfrac{1}{12}$.

237. (C) The exam took $60 + 25 = 85$ minutes to complete. Because the median falls between the third- and fourth-fastest times, the average of the third- and fourth-fastest times is the median. So their sum is two times the median.

$2 * (85 \text{ minutes}) = 170 \text{ minutes}$

238. (D)

I. The average of the 10 numbers is n. *True*, because all the numbers are the same.

II. The median of the 10 numbers is n. *True*, because all the numbers are the same.

III. The median of the 10 numbers is $\dfrac{n}{2}$. *False*, because all the numbers are the same, so the middle number must also be n.

239. (C) The mean will be smaller than 135, but it may or may not be 130. If the numbers are all the same, taking away from the data set would not change the mean. If not, taking away the highest five values will decrease the mean.

240. (C) The total sum of set $\{x_1, x_2, x_3, x_4\}$ is total number of points times the mean $(4 * 3 = 12)$.

The total sum of set $\{y_1, y_2, y_3\}$ is total number of points times the mean $(3 * \text{mean})$

Mean of $\{x_1, x_2, x_3, x_4, y_1, y_2, y_3\} = \dfrac{12 + (3 * \text{mean of } \{y_1, y_2, y_3\})}{7} = 6.$

$12 + (3 * \text{mean of } \{y_1, y_2, y_3\}) = 6 * 7 \Rightarrow \text{mean of } \{y_1, y_2, y_3\} = \dfrac{42 - 12}{3} = 10$

241. (B) 183 out of 225 people had cable $= \dfrac{183}{225}$.

If 600 people were asked, $600 * \dfrac{183}{225} = x \Rightarrow \dfrac{183}{225} = \dfrac{x}{600}$.

242. (C) Probability of A or B happening is $\dfrac{x}{4} + \dfrac{3x}{8} = \dfrac{2x}{8} + \dfrac{3x}{8} = \dfrac{5x}{8}$

243. $\left(\text{Grid-in answer} = \dfrac{64}{3} \right)$

Plug in $y = 8$ to the set: $3y, \dfrac{2}{3}y, 10y,$ and $\dfrac{7}{3}y \Rightarrow 24, \dfrac{16}{3}, 80, \dfrac{56}{3}$

Rearrange to numerical order: $\dfrac{16}{3}, \dfrac{56}{3}, 24, 80$

The median is between $\dfrac{56}{3}$ and $24: \dfrac{\dfrac{56}{3} + 24}{2} = \dfrac{42\dfrac{2}{3}}{2} = 21\dfrac{1}{3} = \dfrac{64}{3}$

244. (Grid-in answer = 1175)

83.90% of the 1400 students participated in viewing activities according to the chart.

$\dfrac{83.90}{100} = \dfrac{x}{1400} \Rightarrow x = \dfrac{83.90}{100} * 1400 = 1174.6 \approx 1175$ students

245. (B) The number 3 in the set will force the mean to be greater than 1. Because there are two or more values of 1 in the set and one value of 3, the median must be 1.

246. (D) The list of five data points starts with 10, has 14 in the middle, and ends in 20.

For the set $\{10, x, 14, y, 20\}$, the mean $= \dfrac{10+x+14+y+20}{5}$ cannot be less than or equal to 13, because

$$\dfrac{10+x+14+y+20}{5} = 13$$
$$10+x+14+y+20 = 65$$
$$x+y = 21$$

So, if $x = 10$, then $y = 11$, which will *not* fit into the set.

If the mean is 14, $\dfrac{10+x+14+y+20}{5} = 14$.

$$10+x+14+y+20 = 70$$
$$x+y = 26$$

So, if $x = 10$, then $y = 16$ which *will* fit into the set.

247. (Grid-in answer $= 124$)

There are 122 consecutive digits between 1 and 124. Thus, there is a 1/122 probability of selecting one of these digits at random. All other ranges with a 1/122 probability would have a greater value for y.

248. (B) $\dfrac{170}{15} = 11.\overline{33} \Rightarrow$ You can go to 11 basketball games without buying the season pass, and the cost ($15 * 11 = 165) would still be less than the $170 season pass.

249. (C) The list must increment by 10, start at 15, and be 8 numbers long.

The list must be $\{15, 25, 35, 45, 55, 65, 75, 85\}$. The median falls between 45 and 55.

$$\therefore \dfrac{45+55}{2} = 50$$

250. (A) The answer can be deduced by considering the scale of the map. If 1 cm on the map is equal to 18 km, then the distance on the map will be $\dfrac{234}{18} = 13$.

251. (D) $1 - \dfrac{2}{9} = \dfrac{7}{9}$

252. (B) Total $= 3+2+10 = 15$

$$\dfrac{\text{Sophomores}}{\text{Total}} = \dfrac{2}{15}$$

253. (B) $\dfrac{\sqrt{2}+5\sqrt{2}}{2} = 3\sqrt{2}$

254. $\left(\text{Grid-in answer} = \dfrac{7}{4}\right)$

In a list of 12 numbers, the median is the average of the sixth and seventh numbers. It states the sixth and seven numbers are the same, so both share the same value as the median (7/4).

255. (D) If they buy six single lessons for $45 each, the total is $270.

That means they will save $270 – $200 = $70 from the original $270 with the deal.

$$\frac{70}{270} * 100 = 25.9\% \approx 26\%$$

256. (Grid-in answer = 12)

The median is $29/2 = 14.5$, meaning the average of the third and fourth number is 14.5. Because the numbers are consecutive, the third and fourth numbers will be 14 and 15. The set will be {12, 13, 14, 15, 16, 17} with a first value of 12.

257. (B) The ratio of red to green is 2:3. That means for every five marbles there are two red marbles.

$$\frac{2}{5} * 800 = 320$$

258. (A) $75\% = 0.75$ and $20\% = 0.20$

$x * 0.75 * 0.20 = x * 0.15$

259. (A) $x\% = \dfrac{x}{100} \Rightarrow x\%$ of $125 = \dfrac{x}{100} * 125 = \dfrac{5x}{4}$

260. (B) The answer can be obtained by summing all of these probabilities. This means that the following should be performed: $\dfrac{1}{8} + \dfrac{1}{4} + \dfrac{1}{3} + \dfrac{1}{6}$.

This leads to $\dfrac{3+6+8+4}{24} = \dfrac{21}{24} = \dfrac{7}{8}$.

261. (C) $45\% = \dfrac{45}{100} \Rightarrow 45\%$ of $6x + 10y = \dfrac{45}{100} * (6x + 10y) = \dfrac{9}{20}(6x + 10y)$

$$\frac{9}{20}(6x + 10y) = \frac{54x + 90}{20} = \frac{27x + 45y}{10}$$

262. (B) A single piece of the furniture costs $\dfrac{675}{5} = 135$ after the 25% increase in price.

That means 125% of $x = 135$, so $\dfrac{125}{100}x = 135 \Rightarrow x = 135 * \dfrac{100}{125} = \$108.00$

263. (B) $\dfrac{a}{b} = \dfrac{3}{11} \Rightarrow a = \dfrac{3b}{11}$

$\dfrac{a+b}{b} = \dfrac{\dfrac{3}{11}b + b}{b} = \dfrac{3}{11} + 1 = \dfrac{3}{11} + \dfrac{11}{11} = \dfrac{14}{11}$

264. (C) If a number has a nonzero remainder when being divided by k, that simply means it is not divisible by k. $100\% - 40\% = 60\%$ are not divisible $= \dfrac{60}{100} = \dfrac{3}{5}$.

265. (D) Increase of 40%: $x * 140\% = 92 \Rightarrow \dfrac{140}{100}x = 92 \Rightarrow x = 92 * \dfrac{100}{140}$

Decrease by 10%:

$90\% * x = \dfrac{90}{100}x = \dfrac{90}{100}\left(92 * \dfrac{100}{140}\right) = \dfrac{92 * 90}{140} = \dfrac{92 * 9}{14} = \dfrac{46 * 9}{7} = \dfrac{414}{7}$

266. (B) Green(g) + 54 = Blue(b) and $g + b = 200$

$g + (g + 54) = 200 \Rightarrow g = \dfrac{200 - 54}{2} = \dfrac{146}{2} = 73$ green cards

$\left(\dfrac{73}{200}\right)100 = 36.5\%$

267. (C) The ratio is 1:3, so one-fourth of the total students are juniors and three-fourths are seniors. The number of total students must be divisible by 4. The only answer choice that is *not* divisible by 4 is 58.

268. (Grid-in answer = 152)

140.60 increases by 3% in the first year: $140.60 * 1.03 = 144.82$

144.82 increases by 5% in the second year: $144.82 * 1.05 = 152.06 \approx \$152$

269. (D) $\dfrac{1}{4}\%x = 19 \rightarrow \dfrac{1/4}{100}x = 19$

$\dfrac{1}{400}x = 19 \rightarrow x = (19)(400) = 7600$

270. (C) To be directly proportional, the relationship is a line with no y-intercept:

$y = mx \rightarrow$ plugging in $x = \sqrt{2}$ and $y = 4$:

$4 = m\sqrt{2} \rightarrow m = 4/\sqrt{2} = 2\sqrt{2}$

Therefore, $y = 2\sqrt{2}x$.

271. (A) Only two of the four lines shown are linear, thus ruling out answer choices (B) and (D). Of the remaining choices, one line has a value of $x = 0$ when $y = -3$, which corresponds to answer choice (A).

272. **(D)** 85% will be paid for the apples during the sale before the coupon for a price of $\dfrac{85}{100}x$.

With a 2% coupon discount, 98% of this amount will be paid:

$$\left(\frac{98}{100}\right)\left(\frac{85}{100}x\right)=\left(\frac{49}{50}\right)\left(\frac{17}{20}x\right)=\left(\frac{833}{100}x\right)$$

273. **(B)** $x>\dfrac{1/8}{100}(2115)$

$x>2.64$

3 is the smallest integer value of x that satisfies this inequality.

274. **(B)** $\dfrac{3\text{ miles}}{20\text{ min}}(100\text{ min})=15\text{ miles}$

$\dfrac{3\text{ miles}}{25\text{ min}}(100\text{ min})=12\text{ miles}$

$15\text{ miles}-12\text{ miles}=3\text{ miles}$

275. (Grid-in answer = 10)

$$\left(\frac{34.90-31.41}{34.90}\right)*100=10\%$$

276. **(C)** $0.06*x=0.87$

$x=\dfrac{0.87}{0.06}=\$14.50$

277. **(D)** Tutor A's rate $=\dfrac{\$90}{3\text{ hours}}=\$30/\text{hour}$

Ratio $=\dfrac{\text{Tutor A's rate}}{\text{Tutor B's rate}}=\dfrac{\$30/\text{hour}}{\$40/\text{hour}}=\dfrac{3}{4}$

278. (Grid-in answer = 18)

For a direct proportion between m and n:

$m=Cn$, where C is a constant

$C=\dfrac{m}{n}=\dfrac{6a}{a}=6$

$m=6n=6(3)=18$

279. (Grid-in answer = 52)

For a direct proportion between b and $a^2 + 1$:

$b = C(a^2 + 1)$, where C is a constant

$$C = \frac{b}{a^2 + 1} = \frac{10}{2^2 + 1} = 2$$

$$b = 2(a^2 + 1) = 2(5^2 + 1) = 52$$

280. **(C)** Right triangles A and B are similar because all their angles are the same.

Since the hypotenuse of A is 4 times the hypotenuse of B, then the height and base of triangle A are both 4 times greater than the height and base of triangle B.

$$\frac{\text{Area}_A}{\text{Area}_B} = \frac{\frac{1}{2}(4h * 4b)}{\frac{1}{2}(h * b)} = \frac{16}{1}$$

281. **(C)** If John won the race by 1,254 votes, then this difference is also the difference between his percentage and that of his opponent because all the votes were cast and counted. This means that John's opponent won $100\% - 56\% = 44\%$ of the vote, and this means that $56\% - 44\% = 12\%$.

This percentage difference is equal to John's margin of victory, which is 1,254 votes.

$1254 = 12\%$ of the votes, which means that the entire number of votes is $1254 * \frac{100}{12} = 10{,}450$.

282. **(A)** $a = x - 0.12x = 0.88x$
$b = x + 0.10x = 1.10x$
$a - b = 0.88x - 1.10x = (0.88 - 1.10)x = -0.22x$

283. **(C)** $\dfrac{3x + 5x + (2x - 1) + (x + 1)}{4} = 8$

$11x = 32$

$x = \dfrac{32}{11}$

$\dfrac{x + (x + 2)}{2} = \dfrac{2x + 2}{2} = x + 1 = \left(\dfrac{32}{11} + 1\right) = \dfrac{43}{11}$

284. **(A)** Area of a single face $= x^2$

Volume of the cube $= x^3$

$\dfrac{\text{Area}}{\text{Volume}} = \dfrac{x^2}{x^3} = \dfrac{1}{x}$

285. **(A)** $\dfrac{m}{n} = \dfrac{2}{9}$

$\dfrac{18m}{n} = 18\left(\dfrac{m}{n}\right) = 18\left(\dfrac{2}{9}\right) = \dfrac{4}{1}$

286. (D) Let $r =$ the number of red marbles and $b =$ the number of blue marbles.

$r = b + 0.15b = 1.15b$

Total marbles $= r + b = (1.15b) + b = 2.15b$

Since the number of marbles is an integer, the total number of marbles must be divisible by 2.15.

The only answer choice evenly divisible by 2.15 is 430.

287. (Grid-in answer = 48)

Since t is inversely proportional to r, then $t = \dfrac{C}{r}$, where C is a constant.

Solving for $C \rightarrow C = tr = (6)(2) = 12$

$t = \dfrac{C}{r} = \dfrac{12}{\dfrac{1}{4}} = 48$

288. (Grid-in answer = 280)

$0.25x - 0.20x = 14$

$0.05x = 14$

$x = \dfrac{14}{0.05} = 280$

289. (C) Let $F =$ Frank's hourly pay and $R =$ Rich's hourly pay.

$\dfrac{F}{R} = \dfrac{5}{6} \rightarrow F = \dfrac{5}{6}R$

$2F + 2R = 66 \rightarrow 2\left(\dfrac{5}{6}R\right) + 2R = 66$

$\dfrac{5}{3}R + \dfrac{6}{3}R = 66 \rightarrow \dfrac{11}{3}R = 66 \rightarrow R = \$18/\text{hour}$

290. (C) Since y and x are inversely proportional, then $y = \dfrac{C}{x}$, where C is a constant.

Plugging in $x = 12n$ and $y = \dfrac{1}{3}n \rightarrow 12n = \dfrac{C}{\dfrac{1}{3}n} \rightarrow C = 4n^2$

Plugging in $C = 4n^2$ and $x = 2n$ in the original expression $\rightarrow y = \dfrac{4n^2}{2n} = 2n$

291. (D) $\left(\dfrac{x}{100}\right)y = \left(\dfrac{y}{100}\right)x = a$

292. (B) Let $X =$ one side of the full-sized garden.

$X^2 = 62{,}500 \text{ ft}^2 \rightarrow X = \sqrt{62{,}500} = 250 \text{ ft}$

Each side of the scale model is one-hundreth of 250 ft $= 2.5$ ft.

The area of the scale model $= (2.5 \text{ ft})^2 = 6.25 \text{ ft}^2$.

293. (A) $\dfrac{x \text{ nails}}{6 \text{ hours}}(20 \text{ hours}) = \dfrac{20x}{6} \text{ nails} = \dfrac{10x}{3} \text{ nails}$

294. (B) $\dfrac{\text{Employees}}{\text{People}} = \dfrac{20}{850} = \dfrac{\text{Employees}}{340}$

$\text{Employees} = \left(\dfrac{20}{850}\right)(340) = 8$

295. (B) $\dfrac{5 \text{ ten-dollar bills}}{15 \text{ one-dollar bills}} = \dfrac{1 \text{ ten-dollar bills}}{3 \text{ one-dollar bills}}$

296. (C) The percentage who now say green is their favorite color:

$\% = \left(\dfrac{\text{Current green lovers}}{\text{Total population}}\right)*100 = \left(\dfrac{x-3}{y}\right)*100 = \dfrac{100(x-3)}{y}$

297. $\left(\text{Grid-in answer} = \dfrac{1}{4} \text{ or } 0.25\right)$

$\text{Probability} = \dfrac{\text{Number of favorable outcomes}}{\text{Total number of outcomes}} = \dfrac{\text{Number of Ns}}{\text{Total number of letters}} = \dfrac{3}{12} = \dfrac{1}{4}$

298. (C) $\dfrac{(x+y)}{100}\left(\dfrac{50}{x^2+2xy+y^2}\right) = \dfrac{(x+y)}{2}\left(\dfrac{1}{(x+y)^2}\right) = \dfrac{1}{2(x+y)}$

299. (B) $\dfrac{(100-64)}{100} = \dfrac{36}{100} = \dfrac{9}{25}$

300. $\left(\text{Grid-in answer} = \dfrac{51}{2} \text{ or } 25.5\right)$

$\dfrac{a}{b} = \dfrac{3}{17} \rightarrow 17a = 3b \rightarrow b = \left(\dfrac{17}{3}\right)a$

Plugging in $a = \dfrac{9}{2} \rightarrow b = \left(\dfrac{17}{3}\right)\dfrac{9}{2} = \dfrac{51}{2}$

301. (D) Let a = original antique value.
After the first year, the value $= a - 0.08a = 0.92a$.
During the second year, the value decreases 2%, or is 98% of its previous value.
$0.98(0.92a) = 0.9016a \approx 0.902a$
The final value is 90.2% of the original.

302. (B) $250 + 0.08(250) = 270$ members

303. **(C)** On sale, item A $= \dfrac{100-10}{100} m = \dfrac{9}{10} m$ and item B $= \dfrac{100-20}{100} n = \dfrac{8}{10} n.$

The total cost $= \dfrac{9}{10} m + \dfrac{8}{10} n = \dfrac{9m+8n}{10}$

304. **(A)** $x = \dfrac{5}{100}\left(\dfrac{1}{4}\right) = \dfrac{1}{80}$

305. (Grid-in answer = 85)

Since 10% are small and 40% are medium, that means 50% of the stock are large.

$\left(\dfrac{50}{100}\right) 170$ jackets $= 85$ jackets

306. **(B)** Because $\dfrac{1}{8} = 0.125 \rightarrow 0.125 y = x$

This may be expressed as 12.5% of $y = x$.

307. **(A)** Because the 37 turtles that made it to the ocean also had to hatch, the probability is

Probability $= \dfrac{\text{Number of favorable outcomes}}{\text{Number of possible outcomes}} = \dfrac{\text{Number of ocean turtles}}{\text{Number of eggs}} = \dfrac{37}{90}$

308. $\left(\text{Grid-in answer} = \dfrac{5}{2} = 2.5\right)$

$\dfrac{x}{y} = \dfrac{1}{3} \rightarrow 3x = y \rightarrow 3x = x+1 \rightarrow 2x = 1 \rightarrow x = \dfrac{1}{2}$

$\dfrac{x}{z} = \dfrac{1}{5} \rightarrow z = 5x \rightarrow z = 5\left(\dfrac{1}{2}\right) = \dfrac{5}{2}$

309. **(C)** The speed of the particle $= \dfrac{4 \text{ units}}{20 \text{ min}} = \dfrac{1 \text{ unit}}{5 \text{ min}}$

The position on the x-axis $= \left(\dfrac{1 \text{ unit}}{5 \text{ min}}\right)(50 \text{ min}) = 10 \text{ units}$

Because there is no motion in the y-direction and the particle started at the origin, the position is (10, 0).

310. **(D)** The slope of the best-fit line is the average rate of change.

Picking two points on the best-fit line (0.25, 1) and (1.5, 4):

$m = \dfrac{\text{Rise}}{\text{Run}} = \dfrac{4-1}{1.5-0.25} = \dfrac{3}{1.25} = \dfrac{3}{(5/4)} = \dfrac{12}{5}$

Section 3

311. (C) Given: $xy^2 = 4$

$$\frac{2x^3y^4 - x^2y^2}{x^2y^2} = \frac{2x^3y^4}{x^2y^2} - \frac{x^2y^2}{x^2y^2} = 2xy^2 - 1 = 2(4) - 1 = 7$$

312. (A) $9m - 6m + 1 = (9 - 6)m + 1 = 3m + 1$

313. (C) $2x^2 - y + 1 = 15 \rightarrow 2x^2 - y = 14$

$\therefore (2x^2 - y) - 7 = (14) - 7 = 7$

314. (C) $\left(\frac{1}{5}x - y\right)^2 = \left(\frac{1}{5}x - y\right)\left(\frac{1}{5}x - y\right) = \frac{x^2}{25} - \frac{2xy}{5} + y^2$

315. (A)

I. $(a - b)^2 = (a^2 - 2ab) + b^2 \rightarrow$ Since $b^2 > 0$, this expression is *always* greater than $a^2 - 2ab$.

II. $a(a - 2b) = (a^2 - 2ab) \rightarrow$ Because of the equality, this option is eliminated.

III. $(a - 2b) \rightarrow$ Because $(a^2 - 2ab) = a(a - 2b)$, $(a - 2b)$ could be $\leq a(a - 2b)$ if $a < 1$.

316. (A) $ab^3 - ab^4 + a^2b^2 = a(b^3 - b^4 + ab^2) = ab(b^2 - b^3 + ab)$

317. (D)

The first function has two nondistinct zeros at $x = 0$.
The second function has three nondistinct zeros at $x = 0$.
The third function has two nondistinct zeros at $x = 4$, and one distinct zero at $x = 0$.
The fourth function has three distinct zeros at $x = -4$, $x = 0$, and $x = 4$.

318. (A)

Mapping $f(x) = -x^2 - 5$ to the form $ax^2 + bx + c$ gives $a = -1$, $b = 0$, and $c = -5$.

To find the x-coordinate of the vertex, $x = \frac{-b}{2a} = \frac{0}{2(-1)} = 0$

$f(0) = -0^2 - 5 = -5$

319. (C) $a^3 = 0$ and $(a^2 - 1) = 0$ are both possibilities for the product to be 0.
That means $a = 0$, $a = 1$, and $a = -1$ are all possible solutions.

320. (C) $f(x) = x^2 - x$
$$f(c+1) = (c+1)^2 - (c+1)$$
$$f(c+1) = c^2 + 2c + 1 - c - 1 = c^2 + c$$

321. (Grid-in answer = 5)
$$3x^2 - 16x + 5 = 0$$
$$(3x - 1)(x - 5) = 0$$
$x = \dfrac{1}{3}$ and $x = 5$ are solutions. The larger value of x is 5.

322. (A) $g(x) = \dfrac{x-6}{x^2}$
$$g(-1) = \frac{-1-6}{(-1)^2} = \frac{-7}{1} = -7$$

323. (D) $f(x) = x + 5$
$$f\left(\frac{1}{8}k + 6\right) = \left(\frac{1}{8}k + 6\right) + 5 = \frac{1}{8}k + 11$$

324. (A) $f(x - 2)$ shifts a graph to the right 2 units.
$f(x + 2)$ shifts a graph to the left 2 units.
$f(x) - 2$ shifts a graph down 2 units.
$f(x) + 2$ shifts a graph up 2 units.

325. (A) $f(1) = -2$ and $f(3) = 5$
$f(1) + f(3) = -2 + 5 = 3$

326. (D) $a > 0$ applies to all parabolas opening up, and this is *true* for our graph.
$b \neq 0$ yields a parabola that is not symmetric about the y-axis,
which is *true* for our graph.
If $c = 0$, then $(0, 0)$ must be a point on the function,
which is *false* for our graph.

327. (D) Any time the function is above the x-axis, $g(x) > 0$.
This is true in the ranges from $-3 < x \leq -2$ and $x > 0$.

328. (D) Beginning with the intercept form of the quadratic equation:
$f(x) = a(x - m) * (x - n)$ and plugging in the x-intercepts:
$f(x) = a(x + 3)(x - 4)$
Using the point $(0, 12)$, $f(0) = a(0 + 3)(0 - 4) = 12$
$-12a = 12 \rightarrow a = -1$
Expanding $f(x) = (-1)(x + 3)(x - 4) = -x^2 + x + 12a$
This mirrors the form $ax^2 + bx + c \therefore b = 1$.

329. (D) Since $f(x) = x - 8$, then $f(n) = n - 8$.
Testing out $f(2) = 2 - 8 = -6$ and $f(3) = 3 - 8 = -5$,
we see that when $n > 2$, then $f(n) > -6$.

330. (B) If $g(x) = \dfrac{x+1}{x}$ and $g(k + 1) = 3$, then $g(k + 1) = \dfrac{(k+1)+1}{k+1} = 3$.
Cross-multiplying: $k + 2 = 3(k + 1)$
$k + 2 = 3k + 3 \rightarrow -1 = 2k \rightarrow k = -\dfrac{1}{2}$

331. (D) $k(1) = 6$ because $x = 1$ is odd
$k(2) = 4$ because $x = 2$ is even
$k(1) + k(2) = 6 + 4 = 10$

332. (A) Since the quadratic function does not cross the x-axis and the point $(0, -4)$
is below the x-axis, the quadratic must open down, so $a < 0$ and only options
(A) and (B) are possible. When $x = 0$, $f(0) = -4$, and between options
(A) and (B), only (A) satifies this criterion.

333. (C) Because the value of the minimum seen on the chart is $(0, 2)$, we can eliminate
any other answer choice except (C).

334. (D) $g(x) = f(x) - 1 = \left(\dfrac{1}{3}x + 5\right) - 1 = \dfrac{1}{3}x + 4$
The slope of $g(x)$ is $\dfrac{1}{3}$.

335. (D) $A = (-k, 0)$ is a point on the function $h(x) = x^2 - 8$.
$\therefore h(-k) = (-k)^2 - 8 = 0$.
Solving for $k \rightarrow k = \pm\sqrt{8} = \pm 2\sqrt{2}$.
The base of the triangle is $2k = 4(\sqrt{2})$, and the height of the triangle is 5:
Area $= \dfrac{1}{2}$(base)(height) $= \dfrac{1}{2}(4\sqrt{2})(5) = 10\sqrt{2}$

336. (C) $f(n) = n^4 - 4n$
$f(-1) = (-1)^4 - 4(-1) = 1 + 4 = 5$

337. (B) Compared to $g(x)$, $h(x) = g(x) - k$ tranforms the function down k units
on the y-axis. Therefore, the point $(-1, 5)$ will shift to $(-1, 5 - k)$.

338. **(C)** Because the functions intersect, $f(x) = g(x) \rightarrow x^2 + 1 = kx^2$.

Plugging in $x = \dfrac{\sqrt{2}}{2} \rightarrow \left(\dfrac{\sqrt{2}}{2}\right)^2 + 1 = k\left(\dfrac{\sqrt{2}}{2}\right)^2$

$\dfrac{1}{2} + 1 = k\left(\dfrac{1}{2}\right) \rightarrow \dfrac{3}{2} = \dfrac{k}{2} \rightarrow k = 3$

339. **(C)** $f(x) = 3x^2 - 4 \therefore g(x) = \dfrac{1}{2}f(x) + 4 = \dfrac{1}{2}(3x^2 - 4) + 4 = \dfrac{3x^2}{2} + 2$

$g(4) = \dfrac{3(4)^2}{2} + 2 = 24 + 2 = 26$

340. **(D)** The maximum of a downward-opening quadratic function is found at $h = \dfrac{-b}{2a}$.
Since $a = -1$ and $b = 12$, the maximum is found at $h = \dfrac{-12}{2(-1)} = 6$.

$c(h) = -h^2 + 12h \rightarrow c(6) = -(6)^2 + 12(6) = 36$

341. **(B)** $V(8) = 5000(0.92)^8 = \$2566.09$

342. (Grid-in answer $= 27$)
$f(x) = x^3 + x^2 - n$
Because the point (3, 9) lies on the function, $f(3) = 9$.
$9 = 3^3 + 3^2 - n$
$9 = 36 - n$
$n = 27$

343. **(C)** Given $h(x) = \dfrac{x-1}{4}$, then $h(x+3) = \dfrac{(x+3)-1}{4} = \dfrac{x+2}{4}$.
Since $h(x+3) = 5$:
$\dfrac{x+2}{4} = 5 \rightarrow x + 2 = 20 \rightarrow x = 18$

344. **(D)** $f(x-6)$ shifts the function $f(x)$ six units to the right.
Thus, the point (4, 0) will become (10, 0).

345. **(B)** The zeros of the function are $x = 4, x = -1, x = -6$, and $x = 9$.
Choice (C), $x = -4$, is not a zero of the function.

346. **(C)** $x = 0$ and $x = 1$ are the only unique zeros of the function, so there are *two* unique values.

347. (Grid-in answer $= 5$)
$f(x) = x^2 - 4x - 5 = (x+1)(x-5)$
The zeros are $x = -1$ and $x = 5$.
The larger zero is $x = 5$.

348. (D) Given that the x value is equal to -1 when they intersect, one way to solve the problem is to input the value into the $f(x)$ equation. When these values are placed, we can identify the following:

$2 = 1 - 2 + n$
$n = 3$

349. (D) Both points satisfy the function: $f(x) = x^2 - 4x - 12$.
$(-2, 0) \rightarrow f(-2) = (-2)^2 - 4(-2) - 12 = 0$
$(6, 0) \rightarrow f(6) = (6)^2 - 4(6) - 12 = 0$

350. (A) $f(x) = \dfrac{4}{5}x^2$ and $g(x) = \dfrac{1}{2}x + \dfrac{1}{2}$

$g(f(x)) = \dfrac{1}{2}\left(\dfrac{4}{5}x^2\right) + \dfrac{1}{2} = \dfrac{2}{5}x^2 + \dfrac{1}{2}$

351. (D) Since all the y-values on the graph are 3 units or less, $f(x) < 4$.

352. (D) $f(x) = -x^2 + 1$ is a parabola opening downward with the maximum at $x = 0$. A vertical translation will only move the parabola up or down along the y-axis, so the maximum will be at $g(0)$.

353. (C) $k(x) = x^3(x^2 - 4x + 4) = x^3(x - 2)(x - 2) = 0$
$x = 0$ and $x = 2$ are the unique zeros of the function.

354. (D)
$n^2 - 8n = 9 \rightarrow n^2 - 8n - 9 = 0 \rightarrow (n - 9)(n + 1) = 0$
$n = 9$ and $n = -1$ are the two solutions.
If $a = 9$, then for b to be distinct, $b = -1$.
$a + b = 9 + (-1) = 8$

355. (C) In order for $f(x) > 0$, all the values on the y-axis must be greater than 0. This is true in the range $-2 < x < 2$.

356. (B) When $a > 0$, the graph is a parabola that opens up with a single minimum value at the vertex. Because c (the y-intercept) can be any value, the parabola may or may not cross the x-axis.

357. (A) Set $h(x) = x^2 + 3x - 8$ and $k(x) = -4$ equal to find the intersection points:
$x^2 + 3x - 8 = -4 \rightarrow x^2 + 3x - 4 = 0 \rightarrow (x + 4)(x - 1) = 0$
$x = 1$ and $x = -4$, and the larger value is $x = 1$

358. (C) Substiute $f(x) = 3x$ into $5f(x) = f(x)$:
$5(3x) = 3x \rightarrow 15x - 3x = 0 \rightarrow 12x = 0 \rightarrow x = 0$

359. (D) $g(m) = 2m - m^3$
$g(-2) = 2(-2) - (-2)^3 = -4 - (-8) = -4 + 8 = 4$

360. (A) For a parabola to have a minimum, it must open upward. If $a > 1$, then the parabola will open upward.

361. (D) $f(x+2)$ shifts a graph 2 units to the left.
$f(x-2)$ shifts a graph 2 units to the right.
$f(x)+2$ shifts a graph 2 units upward on the y-axis.
$f(x)-2$ shifts a graph 2 units downward on the y-axis.

362. (D) $f(x) = \dfrac{x^2 - x}{2}$
$$f(2a-1) = \frac{(2a-1)^2 - (2a-1)}{2} = \frac{4a^2 - 4a + 1 - 2a + 1}{2}$$
$$f(2a-1) = \frac{4a^2 - 6a + 2}{2} = 2a^2 - 3a + 1$$

363. (A) $f(c) = 2c - 9$ and $c > 0$
$2c$ must be positive, so $(2c-9) > -9$

364. (D) There are several ways of solving this task, including sketching the 4 possible functions.

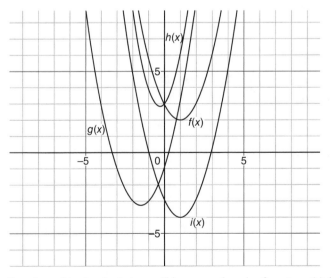

Based on this sketch, it is possible to see that the function $i(x)$ has the smallest minimum.

365. (Grid-in answer = 24)

$$f(t) = -2t^2 + 32$$
$$f(2) = -2(2)^2 + 32 = -8 + 32 = 24 \text{ meters}$$

366. (C) $g(x) = x^3 - kx + c$
$$g(-1) = 4$$
$$(-1)^3 - k(-1) + c = 4$$
$$-1 + k + c = 4$$
$$k + c = 5$$

367. (Grid-in answer = 6)

Given the x-intercepts of a quadratic $m = -1$ and $n = -2$:
$$f(x) = a(x - m)(x - n) = a(x + 1)(y + 2)$$
The last data point on the table is $f(0) = 2$, which plugged in the expression above:
$$f(0) = a(0 + 1)(0 + 2) = 2a$$
$$2 = 2a \rightarrow a = 1$$
Thus, $f(x) = 1(x + 1)(x + 2) = x^2 + 3x + 2$
$$a = 1, b = 3, c = 2$$
The product $bc = (3)(2) = 6$.

368. (C) $f(x) = -x^2 + 10x - 21$
$$g(x) = -f(x) = x^2 - 10x + 21$$
$f(x)$ and $g(x)$ intersect where the functions equal:
$$-x^2 + 10x - 21 = x^2 - 10x + 21$$
$$0 = 2x^2 - 20x + 42$$
$$0 = x^2 - 10x + 21$$
$$0 = (x - 7)(x - 3)$$
$x = 7$ and $x = 3 \rightarrow 2$ are solutions.

369. (Grid-in answer = 7)

Given $f(x) = 5x\sqrt{k}$, then $f(\sqrt{k}) = 5(\sqrt{k})\sqrt{k}$.
Also given $f(\sqrt{k}) = 35$.
Setting the two expressions equal $\rightarrow 5(\sqrt{k})\sqrt{k} = 35$
$$5k = 35 \rightarrow k = 7$$

370. (C) $h(x) = 4x^2 - x^3$
$$y = h(3) = 4(3)^2 - (3)^3 = 9$$

371. (D) Given $f(x) = x^2 - 3$ and $f(2m + 1) = 3m$.
$$(2m + 1)^2 - 3 = 3m$$
$$4m^2 + 4m + 1 - 3 = 3m$$
$$4m^2 + m = 2$$

372. (D) Since $g\left(\dfrac{k}{2}\right) = 3k - 2$, it follows that $g(k) = 6k - 2$.
$$g(4k) = 6(4k) - 2 = 24k - 2$$

373. (Grid-in answer = 9)

$$f(2)+f(4)=3+6=9$$

374. **(D)** Since (0, 5) is transformed to $(-5, 5)$, the graph is shifted 5 units to the left but not up or down. This also applies to the transformation of (8, 8) to (3, 8). If $m=5$ and $n=0$, the transformation $k(x+m)+n=k(x+5)$, which is the desired transformation. $m+n=5+0=5$

375. **(D)**

Given $f(a)=a-1$, $g(a)=a-2$, and $\dfrac{1}{6}f(a)=\dfrac{1}{g(a)}$.

$$\frac{1}{6}(a-1)=\frac{1}{a-2}\to(a-1)(a-2)=6$$
$$a^2-3a+2=6\to a^2-3a+-4=0$$
$$(a-4)(a+1)=0\to a=4\text{ and }a=-1$$

376. **(B)** $f(x)=(x-3)^2+4=x^2-6x+9+4=x^2-6x+13$

377. **(C)** $k(x)=\dfrac{3}{2}$

$$\frac{1}{2}(x-1)^2=\frac{3}{2}\to(x-1)^2=3$$

Taking the square root of both sides:

$$x-1=\pm\sqrt{3}\to x=1\pm\sqrt{3}$$

In order that $x>0$, $x=1+\sqrt{3}$

378. **(A)** $f(x)=cx^3$

Given the point $(-2, 8)$ is on the function:

$$f(-2)=8$$
$$c(-2)^3=8$$
$$-8c=8\to c=-1$$

379. **(B)**

I. "There is no value x such that $f(x)=0$." This is *not* necessarily true if the function is below $y=2$.

II. "There is no value x such that $f(x)=2$." This must be *true*, since we know the function never intersects the line $y=2$.

III. "The function is undefined at the point $x=2$." This may or may not be true, depending on the unique function.

380. (Grid-in answer = 24)

Given $g(x)=\dfrac{f(x)}{8}$ and $g(a)=3$

$$\frac{f(a)}{8}=3\to f(a)=24$$

381. **(B)** Given $g(x) = \dfrac{|x-1|}{x-1}$ and $x > 1$.

$x > 1$ demands that $|x-1|$ is positive, so the absolute value may be removed.

$$g(x) = \frac{x-1}{x-1} = 1$$

382. **(D)** Given: $f(12) = 11$, so all that is known is the point $(12, 11)$ on the function. There is not enough information to determine the value of the function anywhere else.

383. **(A)** $g(x) = f(x+1) + 4$ transforms $f(x)$ by 1 unit to the left and 4 units up.

384. (Grid-in answer = 18)

Given $f(b) = b + b^2 \rightarrow f(2) = 2 + 2^2 = 6$

$$\frac{(f(2))^2}{2} = \frac{6^2}{2} = 18$$

385. **(C)** Given $f(x) = -x^2 + 9$ and $g(x) = x^2 - 9$, the graphs will intersect at

$-x^2 + 9 = x^2 - 9 \rightarrow 2x^2 = 18 \rightarrow x = \pm 3$

Because $x > 0$, $x = 3$

$f(3) = -3^2 + 9 = 0$, so $y = 0$

$x + y = 3 + 0 = 3$

386. (Grid-in answer = 56)

Given $g(x) = \dfrac{1}{2}f(x) + 6$ and $f(x) = x^2$,

$$g(x) = \frac{1}{2}(x^2) + 6 \rightarrow g(10) = \frac{1}{2}(10^2) + 6 = 56$$

Therefore $b = 56$.

387. **(B)** From the first table, the third data point shows $f(3) = 2$.

Therefore, $g(f(3)) = g(2)$.

Looking up $g(2)$ in the second data table yields a value of -3.

388. **(D)** Given $f(x) = 2x$, it follows that $f(g(x)) = 2g(x)$.

(A) If $g(x) = \dfrac{c}{x}$, the $f(g(x)) = 2g(x) = 2\left(\dfrac{c}{x}\right)$.

(B) If $g(x) = x - c$, the $f(g(x)) = 2g(x) = 2(x - c)$.

(C) If $g(x) = \dfrac{x}{c}$, the $f(g(x)) = 2g(x) = 2\left(\dfrac{x}{c}\right)$.

(D) If $g(x) = cx$, the $f(g(x)) = 2g(x) = 2(cx) = 2cx$.

Given that $x > 1$ and $c > 1$, the last function must be the greatest because its a product of b and c.

389. (C) $(i+i^2+i^3+i^4)=i-1-i+1=0$
$i^5+i^6+i^7+i^8=i^4(i+i^2+i^3+i^4)=0$
$i^9+i^{10}+i^{11}+i^{12}=i^8(i+i^2+i^3+i^4)=0$
This also applies for $13-16$ and $17-20$.
This leaves only $i^{21}+i^{22}+i^{23}=i^{20}(i+i^2+i^3)=(1)(i-1-i)=-1$.

390. (A) $i^5-i^2=(i^2 \cdot i^2 \cdot i)-i^2=(-1)(-1)i-(-1)=i+1$

391. (C)

Column A:
$2x^2-14=18 \rightarrow 2x^2=32 \rightarrow x=16 \rightarrow x=4$
Column B:
$2x^2+14=46 \rightarrow 2x^2=32 \rightarrow x=16 \rightarrow x=4$
The columns yield the same positive value for x.

392. (B)
$y=(x+1)(x-6)-6x^2=x^2-5x-6-6x^2$
$y=-5x^2-5x-6$
The linear term bx in the quadratic function is $-5x$.

393. (B) $2x^2+5x+3=(2x+3)(x+1)$

394. (C)
The point $(0,-2)$ indicates that the y-intercept is -2.
Only choices (A) and (C) have a y-intercept of -2.
Plugging $(-1, 2)$ into choice (A)'s equation: $y=-2(-1)^2+2(-1)-2=-6$
does not give $y=2$.
Plugging $(-1, 2)$ into choice (C)'s equation: $y=2(-1)^2-2(-1)-2=2$
gives $y=2$ as required.
Check: Plugging $(3, 10)$ into choice (C)'s equation: $y=2(3)^2-2(3)-2=10$
gives $y=10$ as required.

395. (A)
The point $(0,-4)$ indicates that the y-intercept is -4.
Only choices (A) and (C) have a y-intercept of -4.
Plugging $(-2, 8)$ into choice (A)'s equation: $y=4(-2)^2+2(-2)-4=8$
give $y=8$ as required.
Check: Plugging $(4, 68)$ into choice (A)'s equation: $y=4(4)^2+2(4)-4=68$
give $y=68$ as required.
Plugging $(-2, 8)$ into choice (C)'s equation: $y=2(-2)^2+4(-2)-4=-4$
does *not* give $y=8$.

396. (A) $\frac{2}{3}t^2 - 7 = 17 \rightarrow \frac{2}{3}t^2 = 24 \rightarrow t^2 = \left(\frac{3}{2}\right)24$

$t^2 = 36 \rightarrow t = \pm 6$

397. (C) Choices (A), (B), and (D) all have x^2 terms that make them quadratics. Choice (C) is a linear equation and *not* a quadratic.

398. (D) $3x^2 - 78 = 114 \rightarrow 3x^2 = 192$

$x^2 = 64 \rightarrow x = \pm 8$

399. (B) Given: $y = -\frac{1}{2}x^2 - x + 8$.

The x-coordinate of the vertex of a parabola is found from $x = \frac{-b}{2a}$.

Plugging in $a = -\frac{1}{2}$ and $b = -1$, $x = \frac{-(-1)}{2\left(-\frac{1}{2}\right)} = \frac{1}{-1} = -1$.

400. (C) The x-intercepts are where $y = 0$.

$-x^2 - 6x + 40 = 0$
$-(x^2 + 6x - 40) = 0$
$-(x + 10)(x - 4) = 0$
$x = -10$ and $x = 4$

401. (A) $-3x^2 + 22x + 93 = 0$

$-(3x^2 - 22x - 93) = 0$
$-(3x - 31)(x + 3) = 0$
$x = \frac{31}{3}$ and $x = -3$

402. (D) $4x^2 - 17x + 13 = 0$

$(4x - 13)(x - 1) = 0$
$x = \frac{13}{4}$ and $x = 1$

403. (C) $(5x^3 + 3x^2 - x + 1) - (2x^3 + x - 5) = 5x^3 + 3x^2 - x + 1 - 2x^3 - x + 5 = 3x^3 + 3x^2 - 2x + 6$

404. (C) $(-x^2 - 5x + 7) + (-7x^2 + 5x - 2) = -8x^2 + 5$

405. (A) The y-intercept comes from the point $(0, 585)$.

Only function $P(x) = 25x^2 - 28x + 585$ satisfies this point.

406. (A) $y = -2(x-2)^2 - 4 = -2(x^2 - 4x + 4) - 4 = -2x^2 + 8x - 8 - 4$

$y = -2x^2 + 8x - 12$

Because $a < 0$, it must be a parabola opening down with a vertex at

$x = \dfrac{-b}{2a} = \dfrac{-8}{2(-2)} = 2$ and $y = -2(2)^2 + 8(2) - 12 = -4$

Alternate solution: $y = -2(x-2)^2 - 4$ is in the vertex form $y = a(x-h)^2 + k$, where (h,k) are the coordinates of the vertex $(2, -4)$.

Since $a < 1$, the graph must be the parabola opening downward with vertex $(2, -4)$.

407. (A) $y = -3(x+2)^2 + 5$ is in the vertex form $y = a(x-h)^2 + k$, where (h,k) are the coordinates of the vertex $(-2, 5)$.

The y-intercept is the value of y where $x = 0 \rightarrow y = -3(0+2)^2 + 5 = -7$.

408. (C) Triangle area $= \dfrac{1}{2}bh = \dfrac{1}{2}(x)\left(\dfrac{1}{2}x + 7\right) = \dfrac{1}{4}x^2 + \dfrac{7}{2}x$

409. (A) $(4x - 9)(7x - 2) = 28x^2 - 63x - 8x + 18 = 28x^2 - 71x + 18$

410. (D) Trapezoid area $= \dfrac{(b_1 + b_2)}{2}h = \dfrac{(2x + 1 + 3x + 3)}{2}(x + 3)$

Area $= \dfrac{(5x + 4)}{2}(x + 3) = \dfrac{5x^2 + 19x + 12}{2} = \dfrac{5}{2}x^2 + \dfrac{19}{2}x + 6$

411. (A) The vertex is the maximum value of the function at the coordinate $(-3, 1)$.

412. (B) The vertex form of a parabola is $y = a(x-h)^2 + k$, where (h, k) are the coordinates of the vertex $(0, 3)$.

Thus, $y = ax^2 + 3$.

Solve for a using the point $(-4, -45)$:

$-45 = a(-4)^2 + 3 \rightarrow -48 = 16a \rightarrow a = \dfrac{-48}{16} = -3$

$y = -3x^2 + 3$

413. (C) $(2x - 9)^2 = (2x - 9)(2x - 9) = 4x^2 - 18x - 18x + 81 = 4x^2 - 36x + 81$

414. (B) $y = (x - 6)(x + 5) = x^2 - x - 30$

The vertex is at $x = \dfrac{-b}{2a} = \dfrac{-(-1)}{2(1)} = \dfrac{1}{2}$.

The value of $y\left(\dfrac{1}{2}\right) = \left(\dfrac{1}{2}\right)^2 - \left(\dfrac{1}{2}\right) - 30 = \dfrac{-121}{4}$.

415. (B) Given $\dfrac{4}{y+9} = \dfrac{6}{y-7}$, cross-multiply to get $4(y - 7) = 6(y + 9)$.

$4y - 28 = 6y + 54 \rightarrow 2y = -82 \rightarrow y = -41$

416. (B) $\dfrac{x^3 - 10x^2 + 9x}{x^2 + 5x - 6} = \dfrac{x(x^2 - 10x + 9)}{(x+6)(x-1)} = \dfrac{x(x-9)(x-1)}{(x+6)(x-1)} = \dfrac{x(x-9)}{(x+6)}$

417. (D) $\dfrac{9x^2}{4x} * \dfrac{16x^3}{x^5} = \left(\dfrac{9x}{4}\right)\left(\dfrac{16}{x^2}\right) = \dfrac{9(4)}{x} = \dfrac{36}{x}$

418. (C) $-15x^2 - 21x = -3x(5x + 7)$

419. (A) When solving the equation, it is equal to $f(x) = x^2 - 6x + 9 + 3x - 3 = x^2 - 3x + 6$.

One option would be to calculate the vertex, but this is not really necessary for this question because answer choices (B) and (C) have a negative slope. Based on the values of b and c, we can eliminate answer choice (D).

420. (B) $x^2 - 2x - 120 = 0$
$(x - 12)(x + 10) = 0$
$x = 12$ and $x = -10$

421. (A) Given: $y = (x - 2)^2 + 4$.
The vertex form of a parabola is $y = a(x - h)^2 + k$,
where (h, k) are the coordinates of the vertex $(2, 4)$.
Since $a = 1 > 0$, the parabola must open up.
Graph A is the parabola with vertex $(2, 4)$ that opens up.

422. (D) $\sqrt{-63} = \sqrt{-9 \cdot 7} = \sqrt{9} \cdot \sqrt{-1} \cdot \sqrt{7} = 3i\sqrt{7}$

423. (D) Given: Vertex at $(3, 6)$ and point on the parabola $(4, 4)$.
The vertex form of a parabola is $y = a(x - h)^2 + k$,
where (h, k) are the coordinates of the vertex.
Plug $x = 4$ and $y = 4$ into $y = a(x - 3)^2 + 6$ and solve for a.
$4 = a(4 - 3)^2 + 6 \rightarrow a = -2$
$y = -2(x - 3)^2 + 6$

424. (A) $x^2 + 11x + 28 = (x + 7)(x + 4)$

425. (B) $x^2 + 10x + 22 = 0 \rightarrow x^2 + 10x = -22$
$x^2 + 10x + \left(\dfrac{10}{2}\right)^2 = \left(\dfrac{10}{2}\right)^2 - 22$
$\left(x + \dfrac{10}{2}\right)^2 = 25 - 22$
$(x + 5)^2 = 3 \rightarrow (x + 5) = \pm\sqrt{3} \rightarrow x = -5 \pm \sqrt{3}$

426. (B) $y = 0$ when the stone will hits the ground.
$-16t^2 + 248 = 0 \rightarrow 16t^2 = 248 \rightarrow t = \sqrt{\dfrac{248}{16}} = 3.94$ seconds

427. (C) The equation can be simplified so that it reads $\dfrac{2(x+3)^2}{3(x+3)}=3$.

By utilizing simplification and multiplying the equation by 3, we can deduce that $2x+6=9$.

This means that $2x=3$ and $x=\dfrac{3}{2}$.

428. (D) $(x+5)(x+1)=0$
$x^2+6x+5=0$

429. (A) $\dfrac{x^2-64}{3x^2} \div (x-8) = \dfrac{x^2-64}{3x^2(x-8)} = \dfrac{(x+8)(x-8)}{3x^2(x-8)} = \dfrac{(x+8)}{3x^2}$

430. (C)

This may be solved using long division of $(x-4)\overline{)x^2+24x-3}$

Alternately, find a common denominator for answer choice (C) to prove it's the answer:

$(x+28)+\dfrac{109}{x-4} = \dfrac{(x+28)(x-4)}{(x-4)}+\dfrac{109}{(x-4)} = \dfrac{x^2+24x-112+109}{(x-4)}$

$=\dfrac{x^2+24x-3}{(x-4)}$

431. (B)

$4x^2+10x-24=0 \rightarrow 2(2x^2+5x-12)=0$

$2(2x+3)(x-4)=0 \rightarrow x=\dfrac{-3}{2}$ and $x=4$

432. (A)

$f(x)=\dfrac{x\sqrt{x^2-1}}{x^2-8}$

$f(8)=\dfrac{8\sqrt{8^2-1}}{8^2-8}=\dfrac{8\sqrt{63}}{56}=\dfrac{\sqrt{63}}{7}=\dfrac{3\sqrt{7}}{7}$

433. (A)

$5\sqrt{7}+\sqrt{448}+\sqrt{175}-\sqrt{63}=5\sqrt{7}+\sqrt{64\cdot7}+\sqrt{25\cdot7}-\sqrt{9\cdot7}$
$=5\sqrt{7}+8\sqrt{7}+5\sqrt{7}-3\sqrt{7}=15\sqrt{7}$

434. (C)

$(3-\sqrt{6})^2=(3-\sqrt{6})(3-\sqrt{6})=9-3\sqrt{6}-3\sqrt{6}+\sqrt{6}\cdot\sqrt{6}$
$=9-6\sqrt{6}+6=15-6\sqrt{6}$

435. (D) $6x^2-4x+8=2(3x^2-2x+4)$

436. (D) The part of the equation $\dfrac{9^x}{3^y}$ can be rewritten as $\dfrac{3^{2x}}{3^y}$, which can then be rewritten as 3^{2x-y}. Based on the value we have from the first equation stating that $2x-y=8$, we can conclude that the correct response is 3^8.

437. (A)

Given: $D = -4p^2 + 152p - 270$.

To find the price of the maximum number of drills, find the vertex:

$$p = \frac{-b}{2a} = \frac{-152}{2(-4)} = \$19$$

438. (C)

Get a common denominator $\rightarrow \frac{4}{5}x + \frac{1}{2}y = 16 \rightarrow \frac{8x+5y}{10} = 16 \rightarrow 8x + 5y = 160$.

Solve the second equation for $x \rightarrow x = 24 - y$.

Substitute into the first equation $\rightarrow 8(24 - y) + 5y = 160$.

Solve for $y \rightarrow 192 - 8y + 5y = 160 \rightarrow 3y = 32 \rightarrow y = \frac{32}{3}$.

Plug y into the second equation, and solve for $x \rightarrow x = 24 - y = 24 - \frac{32}{3} = \frac{40}{3}$.

439. (B) $(2x - 1)(x + 3) = 2x^2 - 1x + 6x - 3 = 2x^2 + 5x - 3$

440. (D) $4x^2 - 4x + 1 = (2x - 1)(2x - 1) = (2x - 1)^2$

441. (D) The zeros are at $y = (x + 1)(x - 2)$.

442. (C) $y = (x + 2)(x - 1) = x^2 + x - 2$

443. (Grid-in answer = 12)

$$18 - \frac{(3x)^{\frac{1}{2}}}{2} = 15 \rightarrow \frac{(3x)^{\frac{1}{2}}}{2} = 3 \rightarrow (3x)^{\frac{1}{2}} = 6$$

Squaring both sides $\rightarrow \left((3x)^{\frac{1}{2}} \right)^2 = 6^2 \rightarrow 3x = 36 \rightarrow x = 12$

444. (C) Given: $(x - 2)^2 = \frac{16}{25}$.

Taking the square root of both sides: $(x - 2) = \pm\sqrt{\frac{16}{25}}$.

$(x - 2) = \pm\frac{4}{5} \rightarrow x = 2 \pm \frac{4}{5} \rightarrow x = \frac{6}{5}$ and $x = \frac{14}{5}$

Section 4

445. **(C)** Angle $ABC = 55°$ is the complement of $BCA = 90° - 55° = 35°$.

Angle BCA and angle BCD are linear angles (i.e., they add up to $180°$),

∴ Angle $BCD = 180° - 35° = \boxed{145°}$.

446. **(B)** Divide the shape into two rectangles: 3×6 and 4×5.

The total area is $18 + 20 = \boxed{38 \text{ square units}}$.

447. **(B)**

The diameter of a circle inscribed in a square is the same as the side length of the square $= 6$.

The radius is half the diameter: $R = \dfrac{6}{2} = 3$ units.

Area $= \pi R^2 = \pi(3)^2 = \boxed{9\pi}$

448. **(B)** The ladder forms a right triangle with the building where the ladder is the hypotenuse ($c = 12$), the height of the building is one leg ($a = x$), and the distance from the bottom of the ladder to the building is the unknown leg (b). Using the Pythagorean theorem:

$c^2 = a^2 + b^2 \rightarrow b = \sqrt{c^2 - a^2} = \sqrt{12^2 - x^2} = \boxed{\sqrt{144 - x^2}}$

449. **(A)** The height of the triangle may be found using the Pythagorean theorem:

Side $BC = 4$ is the hypotenuse, side MC is half of the side length of the equilateral triangle.

$MC = \dfrac{4}{2} = 2$, and the height, MB, is unknown.

$c^2 = a^2 + b^2 \rightarrow b = \sqrt{c^2 - a^2} \rightarrow MB = \sqrt{BC^2 - MC^2} = \sqrt{4^2 - 2^2} = \sqrt{12} = 2\sqrt{3}$.

Because of the symmetry, the perimeter of ABM is the same as the perimeter of CBM.

Perimeter = sum of the sides $= 4 + 2 + 2\sqrt{3} = \boxed{6 + 2\sqrt{3}}$

450. (Grid-in answer $= 3$)

Using the Pythagorean theorem:

$c^2 = a^2 + b^2 \rightarrow (4x - 2)^2 = 6^2 + 8^2$

$16x^2 - 16x + 4 = 100 \rightarrow 16x^2 - 16x - 96 = 0$

Dividing both sides by $16 \rightarrow x^2 - x - 6 = 0$

$(x - 3)(x + 2) = 0 \rightarrow x = 3$ and $x = -2$.

$\boxed{x = 3}$ gives a positive hypotenuse.

Alternate solution: Recognize the triangle as a 3-4-5 triangle with side lengths 6, 8, and 10. Thus $4x - 2 = 10 \rightarrow x = 3$.

451. (Grid-in answer = 54)

Let w = width and $6w$ = length. The perimeter is $w + w + 6w + 6w = 14w$.
$14w = 48 \rightarrow w = 3$
Area = length · width = $w \cdot 6w = 6w^2 = 6(3)^2 = \boxed{54}$

452. **(A)** Since $BC = AC$, triangle ABC is isosceles. The angles across
from the congruent sides are equal, $\therefore \angle CBA = \angle CAB = 70°$
All the angles triangle ABC must add up to 180 degrees:
$\angle BCA = 180° - 70° - 70° = 40°$.
$\angle DCE$ and $\angle BCA$ are vertical angles, and vertical angles are always congruent.
$\therefore \angle DCE = \angle BCA = \boxed{40°}$

453. **(B)** An equilateral triangle has three sides of the same length, so the $\boxed{\text{perimeter is } 3z}$.

454. **(D)** To answer the question, the easiest approach is to begin with the basic equation
that states that $\dfrac{\sin \alpha}{\cos \alpha} = \tan \alpha$.

By substituting the known values, we can determine that $\dfrac{1}{3} = \dfrac{5}{12} \cos \alpha$.

It can be inferred by multiplying by 12 and then dividing by 5 that $\cos \alpha = \dfrac{4}{5}$.

455. **(C)** All sides of the triangle are congruent, so the radius BC of the circle is $\dfrac{x}{2}$.

The area of a half circle $= \dfrac{\pi R^2}{2} = \dfrac{\pi \left(\dfrac{x}{2}\right)^2}{2} = \boxed{\dfrac{\pi x^2}{8}}$

456. (Grid-in answer = 1)

d is the hypotenuse of triangle ABC. Using the Pythagorean theorem:
$d^2 = x^2 + y^2$
Ratio $= \dfrac{d^2}{x^2 + y^2} = \dfrac{x^2 + y^2}{x^2 + y^2} = \boxed{1}$

457. **(C)** $\dfrac{\text{Area}_2}{\text{Area}_1} = \dfrac{\pi R_2^{\,2}}{\pi R_1^{\,2}} = \dfrac{\left(\dfrac{4m}{2}\right)^2}{\left(\dfrac{m}{2}\right)^2} = \dfrac{\dfrac{16m^2}{4}}{\dfrac{m^2}{4}} = \boxed{16}$

458. (A)

    I. "The area of the square is larger than the area of the circle." This must be ***true*** because the circle may be inscribed within the square.

    II. "The perimeter of the square is smaller than the circumference of the circle." This is ***false*** because, given a circle of diameter D, the square has a perimeter of $4D$ and the circle has a circumference of $2\pi \dfrac{D}{2} \approx 3.14D$.

    III. "The radius of the circle is the same as the perimeter of the square." This is definitely ***false*** because the perimeter of the square is $4D$ and the radius of the circle is $\dfrac{D}{2}$.

459. (B) First, the arc length $\overarc{AB}$ must be found. $40°$ is $\dfrac{1}{9}$ of $360°$, so the length of $\overarc{AB}$ is $\dfrac{1}{9}$ of the circumference of the circle.

$$\text{Length}\,(\overarc{AB}) = \frac{1}{9}(2\pi R) = \frac{1}{9}(2\pi 5) = \frac{10}{9}\pi$$

The perimeter of $\triangle AOB = 5 + 5 + \dfrac{10}{9}\pi = \boxed{10 + \dfrac{10\pi}{9}}$

460. (D) Volume of one box $=$ length $*$ width $*$ height $= (2\text{ in}) \cdot (3\text{ in}) \cdot (10\text{ in}) = 60\text{ in}^3$

Since the storage container is completely filled with 40 boxes, the volume is

$40\left(60\text{ in}^3\right) = \boxed{2400\text{ in}^3}$.

461. (A)

The radius of the circle is $R = \dfrac{12}{2} = 6$, and the side of the square is $S = 8$.

Subtract the area of square from the area of the circle to obtain the area of 4 of the shaded regions:

$$\text{Area of one shaded region} = \frac{\text{Area}_{circle} - \text{Area}_{square}}{4} = \frac{\pi 6^2 - 8^2}{4} = \frac{36\pi - 64}{4} =$$

$\boxed{9\pi - 16}$

462. (B)

The missing angle in the triangle on the left $= 180° - 70° - 70° = 40°$.
The missing angle in the triangle on the right $= 180° - 80° - 80° = 20°$.
The four angles on the inside must add up to $360°$:

$$40° + 20° + c + \frac{3}{2}c = 360° \rightarrow \frac{5}{2}c = 300° \rightarrow \boxed{c = 120°}$$

463. (Grid-in answer $= \dfrac{3}{2}$ or 1.5)

$$\frac{\text{Area}_{\triangle ABC}}{\text{Area}_{\triangle DEF}} = \frac{\dfrac{1}{2}b_1 h_1}{\dfrac{1}{2}b_2 h_2} = \left(\frac{b_1}{b_2}\right)\left(\frac{h_1}{h_2}\right)$$

Given: $\triangle ABC$ has twice the area of $\triangle DEF$, $h_1 = 4$, and $h_2 = 3$

$$2 = \left(\frac{b_1}{b_2}\right)\left(\frac{4}{3}\right) \rightarrow \boxed{\left(\frac{b_1}{b_2}\right) = \frac{2(3)}{4} = \frac{3}{2}}$$

464. (A) $\dfrac{\text{Area}_2}{\text{Area}_1} = \dfrac{k(6k)}{k(2k)} \rightarrow \boxed{\dfrac{\text{Area}_2}{\text{Area}_1} = 3}$

465. (B)

The sine of an angle is the ratio of the opposite side of a right triangle to the hypotenuse.

Use the Pythagorean theorem to find the adjacent side to the angle:
$$a = \sqrt{2^2 - 1^2} = \sqrt{3}.$$
The cosine of an angle is the ratio of the adjacent side to the hypotenuse:

$$\boxed{\cos x = \frac{\sqrt{3}}{2}}.$$

466. (D)

Let A_1 be the area of the small half circle and A_2 be the area of the large half circle:
Given $A_1 + A_2 = 40\pi$ and the radius of half circle $R_1 = 4$,

$$\frac{\pi 4^2}{2} + A_2 = 40\pi \rightarrow A_2 = 40\pi - 8\pi = 32\pi$$

$$A_2 = \frac{\pi R_2^{\,2}}{2} = 32\pi \rightarrow R_2^{\,2} = 64 \rightarrow R_2 = 8$$

Length $\overline{AE} = 2R_1 + 2R_2 = 2(4) + 2(8) \rightarrow \boxed{\text{Length } \overline{AE} = 24}$

467. (C)

The total perimeter of the shaded region is $p = \overline{AB} + \overline{BC} + \overline{RC} + \overline{QR} + \overline{PQ} + \overline{AP}$.
In equilateral $\triangle ABC$, $\overline{AB} = \overline{BC} = \overline{AC} = 4$, and in equilateral $\triangle PQR$, $\overline{PQ} = \overline{QR} = \overline{PR} = 2$.
$$\overline{AP} + \overline{RC} = \overline{AC} - \overline{PR} = 4 - 2 = 2$$
$$p = 4 + 4 + \overline{RC} + 2 + 2 + \overline{AP} = 12 + (\overline{AP} + \overline{RC}) = 12 + (2) \rightarrow \boxed{p = 14}$$

468. (C)

The altitude, $\overline{BD}$, of the equilateral triangle bisects $\overline{AC}$ ∴ the length of $\overline{AD} = \dfrac{x}{2}$.

The perimeter of $\triangle ABD = x + \dfrac{x}{2} + h$, where h is the height of the triangle.

h may be found from the Pythagorean theorem: $h = \sqrt{x^2 - \left(\dfrac{x}{2}\right)^2} = \sqrt{\dfrac{4x^2}{4} - \dfrac{x^2}{4}} = \dfrac{\sqrt{3}}{2}x$

$p = x + \dfrac{x}{2} + h = \dfrac{3}{2}x + \dfrac{\sqrt{3}}{2}x \rightarrow \boxed{p = \dfrac{3 + \sqrt{3}}{2}x}$

469. (A) The volume of a rectanguar prism $= lwh = \dfrac{19}{2}$

Solving for $l \rightarrow \boxed{l = \dfrac{19}{2wh}}$

470. (C) $\tan\alpha = \dfrac{\sin\alpha}{\cos\alpha} = \dfrac{\frac{12}{13}}{\frac{5}{13}} = \dfrac{12}{5} \rightarrow \boxed{\tan\alpha = \dfrac{12}{5}}$

471. (D) The interior angles of a quadrilateral add up to $360°$.

∴ $x + y + z + 80° = 360° \rightarrow \boxed{x + y + z = 280°}$

472. (B) The volume of a cube: $s^3 = 27 \rightarrow s = 3m$.

The area of five sides of a cube is $5s^2 = 5(3m)^2 = 45m^2$.

$\dfrac{4 \text{ gallons}}{10m^2}(45m^2) = 18$ gallons $\rightarrow \boxed{18 \text{ gallons required to paint five sides of the cube}}$

473. (Grid-in answer $= 16$)

The 50% increase in area of the original rectangle is $\dfrac{A}{2} = w(8)$,

where w is the width.

$A = 16w \rightarrow lw = 16w \rightarrow \boxed{l = 16}$

474. (B) First find the hypotenuse using the Pythagorean theorem:

Hypotenuse $= \sqrt{3^2 + 4^2} = 5$

$\cos A = \dfrac{\text{Adjacent}}{\text{Hypotenuse}} \rightarrow \boxed{\cos A = \dfrac{4}{5}}$

475. (grid-in answer = 12)

The path length along the two arcs is half the circumference of the circles =
$$\frac{2\pi R}{2} = \pi R.$$

The length of the solid line path $= \overline{AB} + \overparen{BC} + \overline{CD} + \overparen{DE} + \overline{EF}$
$= 2 + \pi(1) + 2 + \pi(1) + 2 = 6 + 2\pi \approx 6 + 2(3)$
$= 12 \rightarrow$ $\boxed{\text{Length of oulined path} = 12}$

476. (Grid-in answer = 20)

The total perimeter of the two equilateral triangles is $3a + 3b = 72$.

Also given: $a = \dfrac{b}{5}$

Substituting: $3\left(\dfrac{b}{5}\right) + 3b = 72$

Getting a common denominator: $\dfrac{3b}{5} + \dfrac{15b}{5} = 72 \rightarrow 18b = 360 \rightarrow \boxed{b = 20}$

477. (**A**)

Angle x and the 35 degree angle are congruent because they are alternate-interior angles about the parallel lines.

Angle y and the 30 degree angle are congruent for the same reason.

$x + y = 35° + 30° \rightarrow \boxed{x + y = 65°}$

478. (**A**) $\sin \angle A = \dfrac{\text{Opposite}}{\text{Hypotenuse}} \rightarrow \boxed{\sin \angle A = \dfrac{1}{2}}$

479. (**A**)

Take away both the interior rectangle and the four small triangles from the area of the big rectangle:

$\text{Area} = 6(3) - 4(3) - 4\left(\dfrac{1}{2}(1)(1)\right) = 18 - 12 - 2 \rightarrow \boxed{\text{Area} = 4 \text{ units}}$

480. (**C**)

$\triangle DEF$ divides $\triangle ABC$ into four congruent equilateral triangles with side lengths of 2.

The height of $\triangle DEF$ may be found using the Pythagorean theorem:

$h = \sqrt{2^2 - 1^2} = \sqrt{3}$

$\text{Area}_{\triangle DEF} = \dfrac{1}{2}(\text{Base})(\text{Height}) = \dfrac{1}{2}(2)\sqrt{3} = \sqrt{3} \rightarrow \boxed{\text{Area}_{\triangle DEF} = \sqrt{3}}$

481. (**A**) The angles in the triangle must add up to 180 degrees.

$\therefore x + y + 85° = 180° \rightarrow y = 180° - 85° - x \rightarrow y = 95° - x$

z and y are linear angles that must be supplementary.

$\therefore z = 180° - y = 180° - (95° - x) = 85° + x \rightarrow \boxed{z = 85° + x}$

482. (D) Define point P at the intersection of $\overline{BD}$ and $\overline{CE}$.

$\angle CBD$ must be $40°$ because it forms a right angle with $\angle ABD = 50°$.

$\triangle BCP$ is a right triangle, so $\angle BPC$ must be $90° - 40° = 50°$.

$\angle BPC$ is colinear with x $\therefore x = 180° - 50° = 130° \rightarrow \boxed{x = 130°}$

483. (C) The triangle is an isosceles right triangle with length x.

Using the Pythagorean theorem: $x^2 + x^2 = \left(3\sqrt{2}\right)^2 \rightarrow 2x^2 = 18 \rightarrow x^2 = 9$

$\text{Area} = \dfrac{1}{2}(\text{Base})(\text{Height}) = \dfrac{1}{2}(x)(x) = \dfrac{1}{2}x^2 = \dfrac{1}{2}(9) = \dfrac{9}{2} \rightarrow \boxed{\text{Area} = \dfrac{9}{2}}$

484. (C) The volume of a cylinder is the area of the base time the height.

$\text{Volume} = A_{\text{Base}}h = \pi R^2 h = \pi(4)^2(10) = 160\pi \rightarrow \boxed{\text{Volume} = 160\pi}$

485. (D) $\sin(53°) = \dfrac{\text{Opposite}}{\text{Hypotenuse}} = \dfrac{\text{Height}}{10}$

$\text{Height} = (10)\sin(53°) \approx 8 \rightarrow \boxed{\text{Length}(\overline{AB}) = 8}$

(Note: Make sure your calculator is in degrees mode.)

486. (D)

The area of the ring is the difference between the area of the large circle and the area of the small circle.

$\text{Area}_{\text{ring}} = \pi(9)^2 - \pi(5)^2 = 56\pi$

The shaded fraction of the ring $= \dfrac{105°}{360°} = \dfrac{7}{24}$.

$\text{Area}_{\text{shaded region}} = \dfrac{7}{24}(56\pi) \rightarrow \boxed{\text{Area}_{\text{shaded region}} = \dfrac{49\pi}{3}}$

487. (A) The opposite angles in a parallelogram are congruent $\therefore \angle ADC = \angle ABC = 95°$

$\angle ADC$ and $\angle CDE$ are collinear $\therefore m\angle CDE = 180° - 95° = 85°$

$x + 55° + 85° = 180° \rightarrow x = 180° - 85° - 55° \rightarrow \boxed{x = 40°}$

488. (D) A square with an area of x^2 has side lengths of x.

The perimeter of the square is $x + x + x + x = 4x$.

489. (A)

The diagonal length, x, of a face of the cube is related to the side length, s, by the Pythagorean theorem:

$s^2 + s^2 = x^2 \rightarrow 2s^2 = x^2 \rightarrow s^2 = \dfrac{x^2}{2} \rightarrow s = \sqrt{\dfrac{x^2}{2}} = \dfrac{x}{\sqrt{2}} = \dfrac{x}{\sqrt{2}}\left(\dfrac{\sqrt{2}}{\sqrt{2}}\right) = \dfrac{x\sqrt{2}}{2}$

$\text{Volume} = s^3 = \left(s^2\right)s = \left(\dfrac{x^2}{2}\right)\left(\dfrac{x\sqrt{2}}{2}\right) \rightarrow \boxed{\text{Volume} = \dfrac{x^3\sqrt{2}}{4}}$

490. (Grid-in answer = 8)

$$\pi\left(\frac{R}{2}\right)^2 = 16\pi \rightarrow \frac{R^2}{4} = 16 \rightarrow R^2 = 64 \rightarrow \boxed{R = 8}$$

491. **(D)** $\text{Area}_{\text{Shaded}} = \text{Area}_{\text{Square}} - \text{Area}_{\text{Quarter Circle}}$

$$\text{Area}_{\text{Shaded}} = (10)(10) - \frac{\pi(10)^2}{4} \rightarrow \boxed{\text{Area}_{\text{Shaded}} = 100 - 25\pi}$$

492. **(C)** $\boxed{\text{Five}}$ unique segments may be formed: $\overline{AB}, \overline{AC}, \overline{AD}, \overline{AE},$ and $\overline{AF}$.

493. (Grid-in answer = 343)

A cube (side length s) has six surfaces, each with a surface area of s^2.
$6s^2 = 294 \rightarrow s^2 = 49 \rightarrow s = 7$
$\text{Volume}_{\text{Cube}} = s^3 = 7^3 \rightarrow \boxed{\text{Volume}_{\text{Cube}} = 343}$

494. **(C)**

First find the length of side $\overline{AC}$ using the Pythagorean theorem:
$\overline{AC} = \sqrt{13^2 - 12^2} = 5$.

$$\tan\angle A = \frac{\text{Opposite}}{\text{Adjacent}} \rightarrow \boxed{\tan\angle A = \frac{12}{5}}$$

495. **(B)** Path length $= \dfrac{\text{Circum}_{R=x}}{2} + \dfrac{\text{Circum}_{R=2x}}{2} = \dfrac{2\pi(x)}{2} + \dfrac{2\pi(2x)}{2} = \pi x + 2\pi x$

$\boxed{\text{Path length} = 3\pi x}$

496. **(C)** $\text{Area}_{\text{Rectangular Garden}} = \text{Area}_{\text{Square Garden}}$
$(9)(16) = x^2 \rightarrow 144 = x^2 \rightarrow \boxed{x = 12}$

497. **(A)** The maximum of a sine function is 1.

$$\sin 2x = 1.0 \rightarrow 2x = \sin^{-1}1.0 \rightarrow x = \frac{\sin^{-1}1.0}{2} = \frac{\pi/2}{2} \rightarrow \boxed{x = \frac{\pi}{4}}$$

$$\left[\text{Note: If using a calculator in degrees mode, } \frac{\sin^{-1}1.0}{2} = \frac{90°}{2}\right.$$

$$\left. = 45° \rightarrow 45°\left(\frac{2\pi \text{ radians}}{360°}\right) = \frac{\pi}{4}.\right]$$

498. **(A)**

For the same height and width, the volume of a rectangular prism is directly proportional to its length.

$\therefore$ Prism B is triple the volume of prism A as follows: $\boxed{\dfrac{\text{Volume}_A}{\text{Volume}_B} = \dfrac{1}{3}}$

499. (D) If $x =$ side of the square, then $A_S = x^2$.

$$P = \frac{C}{\pi} \rightarrow 4x = \frac{2\pi R}{\pi} \rightarrow x = \frac{2R}{4} = \frac{R}{2}$$

$$A_C = \pi R^2 = 4\pi \frac{R^2}{4} = 4\pi \left(\frac{R}{2}\right)^2 = 4\pi x^2$$

Solving for $x^2 \rightarrow x^2 = \boxed{A_S = \frac{A_C}{4\pi}}$

500. (D) $\text{Perimeter}_{\text{Rectangle}} = 18$

$$2x + 4x = 18 \rightarrow 6x = 18 \rightarrow x = 3$$

$\overline{BD}$ is the hypotenuse of $\triangle ABD \rightarrow \text{Length} = \sqrt{x^2 + (2x)^2} = \sqrt{5x^2} =$

$\sqrt{5}x = \sqrt{5}(3) = \boxed{3\sqrt{5}}$

NOTES